PRAISE FOR THE
UNCOMMON JUNIOR HIGH GROUP STUDIES

The *Uncommon* Junior High curriculum will help God's Word to become real for your students.

Larry Acosta
Founder of the Hispanic Ministry Center, Urban Youth Workers Institute

The best junior high/middle school curriculum to come out in years.

Jim Burns, Ph.D.
President of HomeWord (www.homeword.com)

A rich resource that makes genuine connections with middle school students and the culture in which they live.

Mark W. Cannister
Professor of Christian Ministries, Gordon College, Wenham, Massachusetts

A landmark resource for years to come.

Chapman R. Clark, Ph.D.
Professor of Youth, Family and Culture, Fuller Theological Seminary

Great biblical material, creative interaction and *user friendly*! What more could you ask for? I highly recommend it!

Ken Davis
Author and Speaker (www.kendavis.com)

A fresh tool . . . geared to make a lasting impact.

Paul Fleischmann
President and Co-founder of the National Network of Youth Ministries

The *Uncommon* Junior High curriculum capitalizes both GOD and TRUTH.

Monty L. Hipp
President, The C4 Group (www.c4group.nonprofitsites.com)

The *Uncommon* Junior High curriculum is truly cross-cultural.

Walt Mueller
Founder and President, Center for Parent/Youth Understanding (www.cpyu.org)

The creators and writers of this curriculum know and love young teens, and that's what sets good junior high curriculum apart from the mediocre stuff!

Mark Oestreicher
Author, Speaker and Consultant (www.markoestreicher.com)

This is serious curriculum for junior-highers! Not only does it take the great themes of the Christian faith seriously, but it takes junior-highers seriously as well.

Wayne Rice
Founder and Director, Understanding Your Teenager (www.waynerice.com)

The *Uncommon* Junior High curriculum fleshes out two absolute essentials for great curriculum: biblical depth and active learning.

Duffy Robbins
Professor of Youth Ministry, Eastern University, St. Davids, Pennsylvania

It's about time that curriculum took junior-highers and youth workers seriously.

Rich Van Pelt
President of Alongside Consulting, Denver, Colorado

The *Uncommon* Junior High curriculum will help leaders bring excellence to every lesson while enjoying the benefit of a simplified preparation time.

Lynn Ziegenfuss
Mentoring Project Director, National Network of Youth Ministries

FRIENDS
& PEER
PRESSURE

FRIENDS & PEER PRESSURE

KARA POWELL
General Editor

Published by Gospel Light
Ventura, California, U.S.A.
www.gospellight.com
Printed in the U.S.A.

Previously published as Pulse #3: *Friends* in the *Life Issues* track and
Pulse #13: *Peer Pressure* in the *Discipleship* track.

Contributing writers: Kara Powell, Ph.D.; Carla LaFayette;
Virginia Bolenbaugh; Mike and Lesley Johnson.

Library of Congress Cataloging-in-Publication Data
Friends and peer pressure / Kara Powell, general editor.
p. cm. — (Uncommon jr. high group study)
ISBN 978-0-8307-4790-0 (trade paper)
1. Friendship—Religious aspects—Christianity—Study and teaching. 2. Peer pressure—
Religious aspects—Christianity—Study and teaching. 3. Christian education of teenagers.
4. Church group work with teenagers. I. Powell, Kara Eckmann, 1970-
BV4647.F7F745 2009
241'.67620712—dc22
2008054215

Rights for publishing this book outside the U.S.A. or in non-English languages are
administered by Gospel Light Worldwide, an international not-for-profit ministry.
For additional information, please visit www.glww.org, email info@glww.org, or write
to Gospel Light Worldwide, 1957 Eastman Avenue, Ventura, CA 93003, U.S.A.

Contents

How to Use the *Uncommon* Junior High Group Studies

Each *Uncommon* junior high group study contains 12 sessions, which are divided into 2 stand-alone units of 6 sessions each. You may choose to teach all 12 sessions consecutively, or to use just one unit, or to present each session separately. You know your group, so do what works best for you and your students.

This is your leader's guidebook for teaching your group. Electronic files (in PDF format) for each session's student handouts are available online at **www.gospellight.com/uncommon/uncommon_jh_friends_and_peer_pressure.zip**. The handouts include the "Reflect" section of each study, formatted for easy printing, in addition to any student worksheets for the session. You may print as many copies as you need for your group.

Each individual session begins with a brief overview of the "big idea" of the lesson, the aims of the session, the primary Bible verse and additional verses that tie in to the topic being discussed. Each of the 12 sessions is geared to be 45 to 90 minutes in length and is comprised of two options that you can choose from, based on the type of group that you have. Option 1 tends to be a more active learning experience, while Option 2 tends to be a more discussion-oriented exercise.

The sections in each session are as follows:

Starter
Young people will stay in your youth group longer if they feel comfortable and make friends. This first section helps students get to know each other better and focus on the theme of the lesson in a fun and engaging way.

Message
The Message section enables students to look up to God by relating the words of Scripture to the session topic.

Dig

Unfortunately, many young people are biblically illiterate. In this section, students look inward and discover how God's Word connects with their own world.

Apply

Young people need the opportunity to think through the issues at hand. The apply section leads students out into their world with specific challenges to apply at school, at home and with their friends.

Reflect

This concluding section of the study allows students to reflect on the material presented in the session. You can print these pages from the PDF found at **www.gospellight.com/uncommon/uncommon_jh_friends_and_peer_pres sure.zip** and give them to your students as a handout for them to work on throughout the week.

Want More Options?

An additional option for each section, along with accompanying worksheets, is available in PDF format at **www.gospellight.com/uncommon/ uncommon_jh_friends_and_peer_pressure.zip**.

UNIT I
Friends

Why talk with junior-highers about friends? Because it's who they are! It's a core issue in their world. When puberty hits, life changes. I know this is an obvious, oversimplified statement, but it's really the understatement of the century for young teens.

Life for junior-highers is all about change. They're a bundle of physical, emotional, mental, spiritual and relational changes. The world of a young teen is expanding, both as a result of these changes and from attending a school that now draws from a region rather than the local neighborhood. With this personal world-expansion come new friendships, formed around common interests rather than physical proximity.

So, why talk to junior-highers about friends? Because there aren't many things more important to junior-highers than friendship. Their identities are just beginning to form, and junior-highers need to understand the dynamics of true friendship. How do you speak with junior-highers about friends? The subject of friends is so broad—there are a hundred different sessions you could teach, and most junior-highers aren't interested in a 100-week teaching series! Here are a handful of things that are good for junior-highers to understand:

- *God cares about our friendships.* God's not disinterested. He designed relationships, after all. And He desires for us to have healthy, fun, supportive friendships.

- *The best way to have good friendships is to be a good friend.* This sounds a bit cliché, I know, but it's a very true statement that young teens often miss. They can be in a friendship for completely selfish reasons, treat a friend with disrespect and be bossy, and still wonder why it's not a good friendship.

- *Friendships often change as you grow up.* It's okay—even normal—for students to experience changes in their friendships when they move from childhood into their teenage years. Help them to understand that it's not necessarily a failed friendship if they don't still hit it off with their best friend from second grade.

- *Everyone is lonely sometimes.* The biggest friendship issue for some of the students in your group will be that they have no friends. Sometimes this is only a false perception, but sometimes it is the true reality. Help them understand that they aren't freaks or losers. It's tough to develop good friends, and everyone goes through times in life when they have fewer friends than they would like.

Enjoy speaking with your junior-highers about friends. It's one of those rare subjects they will show some interest in!

Kara Powell
Director of the Center for Youth and Family Ministry
Assistant Professor of Youth, Family and Culture
Fuller Theological Seminary

BUILDING FRIENDSHIPS

THE BIG IDEA

Challenging one another by asking hard questions builds friendships.

SESSION AIMS

In this session you will guide students to (1) learn about the strong friendship between Jonathan and David that challenged them both to think and grow; (2) feel the need to build friendships that will challenge them to think and grow; and (3) act by identifying at least one friendship that has the potential to help them grow.

THE BIGGEST VERSE

"Then David fled from Naioth at Ramah and went to Jonathan and asked, 'What have I done? What is my crime? How have I wronged your father, that he is trying to take my life?'" (1 Samuel 20:1).

OTHER IMPORTANT VERSES

1 Samuel 18:7-8; 20:1-4; Proverbs 12:15; Mark 8:27-30; Luke 15:7

Note: Additional options and worksheets in 8½" x 11" format for this session are available for download at **www.gospellight.com/uncommon/jh_friends_and_peer_pressure.zip**.

STARTER

Option 1: Go to the Wall. For this option, you need just this book!

Greet students and explain that you're going to start this new series on friendship by playing Go to the Wall. Ask everyone to stand in the center of the room. (It's best to play this in a room that's not too filled with furniture—perhaps an empty classroom, instead of the youth room that's filled with folding chairs and the refreshment table still covered with remnants of last week's donuts.)

Tell students that you're going to call out four types of food and they need to listen to see which they like the most. As you call out the types of food, assign a wall for each one and tell students to go to that wall. For instance, you might say: "If you like Mexican food, go to that wall; Chinese, go stand at that wall; Italian, go to that wall; and if you prefer Mom's home cookin', go to that wall."

Next, do the same with vacations by asking students which vacation location they would prefer: a tropical beach; a cabin in the mountains; a Paris hotel; an amusement park in Orlando.

Continue the activity with other choices:

- Music styles: country, ska, rock 'n' roll, rap or pop
- Cars: VW Bug, Mercedes convertible, Jeep Wrangler or Porsche
- Fast food: McDonald's, Taco Bell, Subway or Burger King
- Movies: adventure, science fiction, comedy or horror

Add to or change the lists to fit your group.

You'll find that students will enjoy the decision-making and have fun being able to choose whatever they want. They'll also be surprised to see who else in their group ends up at the same wall with them—and who doesn't.

When you're finished, invite students to take their places and ask, "Did anyone feel left out when you went to a wall and some of your friends were at a

Youth Leader Tip

It's fun when, throughout the course of the group meeting, someone says something that is off-the-wall or just funny, you sentence him or her by saying, "Go to the wall!"

different one? Was anyone surprised by the decisions of others? Did any two people here go to all of the same walls together?"

Explain that just as we have different tastes in food, restaurants, cars and music, we often enjoy hanging out with different kinds of friends. There are friends we have that make us laugh and let us goof off. We have friends for talking and sharing secrets. There are "just-for-fun" friends for going to a movie and the mall with. Some of us have those special friends who challenge us and hold us accountable for our actions. There are even "crying-together" friends.

Explain that today, you're going to look at how close friends can challenge us by asking hard and sometimes uncomfortable questions.

Option 2: Word Up. For this option, you need copies of "Word Up" (found on the following page), a bell or buzzer, a stopwatch and 3x5-inch index cards. If you're into prizes, you might want to prepare something for the winning team. Ahead of time, cut apart the cards in the "Word Up" handout. (This game is similar to Charades, except that you talk!)

Greet students and explain that the topic of this new series is friendship. Next, divide the group into two teams. If the numbers work out equally, dividing the group into girls and guys can make for fun, healthy competition. The girls' team chooses someone to go first, and then only that girl is shown a card with a main word written on it in all uppercase letters. This main word is the word that she has to try to get her team to say by using verbal clues, including words, phrases or sentences. Also listed on the card are words that she *cannot use* while trying to get her team members to guess the main word.

The first team member has 20 seconds to get her team to guess the word. If she succeeds, then the next girl on the team gets a card and tries to do the same thing with a different word in 20 seconds or less.

If the first team cannot do it in 20 seconds, the guys' team goes next, repeating the process. Once the second team fails to guess a word within 20 seconds, it's the first team's turn again. As the leader, you need to watch the card closely and listen to the hints being given to the teams. If "forbidden" words are used, ring the bell or buzz the buzzer, and the point and the turn goes to the other team.

After about five minutes or after all the words have been guessed, invite students back to their places and say, "As you can see, saying the wrong words is often very easy to do. Saying the right thing is usually harder to do, and the right words are hard to find. This is also true in our friendships. We often say the wrong words because we don't know what the right words are."

WORD UP

SECRET	FAMILY	COMPUTER	JEANS
whisper	mom	type	blue
tell	dad	internet	pants
private	brother	E-mail	wear
keep	sister	mouse	denim
children	home	screen	legs

FILM	BOOK	MUSIC	SCHOOL
camera	read	listen	class
photo	school	CD player	student
movie	write	iPod	teacher
produce	paper	stereo	learn
color	words	radio	junior high

FRIEND	CAR	COMMERCIAL	CHEWING GUM
time	drive	radio	mouth
pal	steering wheel	television	bubbles
someone	road	sell	pink
buddy	go	jingle	tongue
talk	gasoline	buy	blow

BASKETBALL	MILK	LAMP	CALENDAR
hoop	cookies	light	days
team	nonfat	light bulb	months
court	low fat	read	years
dribble	white	room	plans
players	cereal	lampshade	meetings

Explain that today you're going to look at how friends who ask hard questions and say words that challenge us can really be a good thing for us.

MESSAGE

Option 1: David and Jonathan's Arms. For this option, you need just this fantastic book.

Ask for four volunteers and assign them the following roles: *David, David's arms, Jonathan* and *Jonathan's arms.* Explain that the Bible is full of stories about all kinds of friendships, and you're going to read a portion from probably the most famous friendship in all of the Old Testament.

Instruct the volunteers that they will be acting out a short passage. The two students playing David and Jonathan simply repeat what you (as the narrator) read, but the volunteers playing their arms should act with exaggerated animation in keeping with these particular verbs: "exclaimed," "protested," "fumed" and "begged." The probably hilarious catch is that David and Jonathan must hold their hands behind their backs while the two volunteers playing their arms stand behind them, slipping their arms through to the front to gesture as their talking partner repeats the Scripture verses. (*Note*: Giving the volunteers a few moments of rehearsal might help in making the delivery more creative and lively.)

Next, read the following script adapted from 1 Samuel 20:1-4, making sure to pause long enough to give the arms time to act out the emotions.

> **David** *exclaimed*: (pause) "What have I done? Why is your father so determined to kill me?"
>
> **Jonathan** *protested*: (pause) "That's not true! I'm sure he's not planning any such thing, for he always tells me everything he's going to do, even little things, and I know he wouldn't hide something like this from me. It just isn't so."
>
> **David** *fumed*: (pause) "Of course you don't know about it! Your father knows perfectly well about our friendship, so he has said to himself, 'I won't tell Jonathan—why should I hurt him?' But the truth is that I am only a step away from death! I swear it by the Lord and by your own soul!"
>
> **Jonathan** *begged*: (pause) "Whatever you want me to do, I will do it for you."

When you are finished, thank your Oscar-winning cast—especially the arms—for their creative input in helping demonstrate the way that Scripture can come alive.

Explain that Jonathan and David were the best of friends, and in this passage, David had to inform Jonathan of some disturbing news about Jonathan's father.[1] Their friendship was put to the test, but it passed with flying colors. Read 1 Samuel 20:1-4, and then lead a discussion about the following questions:

- What might have been some of Jonathan's emotions when David told him the disturbing news about his father? *Anger, denial.*
- What were some of David's emotions? *Desperation, anxiety.*
- How is Jonathan's final question a gesture of his loyal commitment (see verse 4)? *He was no longer defending his father and he wanted to know how he could help.*

If students are open to discussing how they would have felt if they had been Jonathan or David, encourage them to share.

Make it clear that Jonathan and David's friendship was strong and special, but strengthened even more as they both took risks and shared the truth. David was the kind of friend who cared enough to tell it like it was, and Jonathan was the kind of friend who was loyal even through the tough times.

Transition to the next point by encouraging students to think of people in their own lives who care enough to speak the truth, even though it might hurt.

Option 2: Bittersweet Friendship. For this option, you need several Bibles, one package of unsweetened baking chocolate (found in your local grocery store's baking aisle) and enough "real" candy (chocolate bars) for everyone. (*Note:* Most unsweetened baking chocolate bars come divided in smaller squares just like a regular chocolate bar; make sure you get enough so that each member in the group receives a small square.)

Youth Leader Tip

Be sensitive to students who may not have many friends in the group, and when the time comes to divide them into small groups, be careful not to pair up a set of best friends with a third person.

Begin by explaining, "We all have different types of friends and we share with them in different ways. Sometimes our most important friendships are built around difficult situations and hard times. Often those times are uncomfortable and sometimes they can be painful, but the friendship sees us through and even helps us learn and grow in the midst of it all."

Next, break the unsweetened chocolate bar into enough individual squares for everyone. Pass the chocolate around and invite each person to take a piece but not to eat it yet. Once all the students have a piece, instruct them to put the chocolate in their mouths at the same time. Their responses should be simultaneous and similar: *Yuck! Eww!*

Apologize for the bitter shock, and as you pass around "real" chocolate, explain that a friendship can be just like bitter chocolate: It seems sweet at a glance, but it can turn bitter and challenging. There is a great story of friendship in the Bible that was bittersweet—namely, the bitterness of trouble and the sweetness of undying friendship between two men. Have students follow along as you read 1 Samuel 20:1-4 aloud. Explain that Jonathan and David were great friends, but this disturbing news had the potential to ruin their relationship.

Discuss the following:

- What did David risk by informing Jonathan about his dad's hatred? *Rejection, losing his friend, angering Jonathan.*
- What did Jonathan risk by pledging his loyal support to David? *He risked his father's love and support, even his own life.*
- Did the conversation here in this passage seem sweet or bitter at first? *Bitter. It turned sweet when Jonathan said, "Whatever you want me to do, I'll do for you" (see verse 4).*

Explain that the friendship between Jonathan and David was strong and special and was strengthened even more as they shared the truth—no matter how hard it may have been for David to share it or Jonathan to hear it.

DIG

Option 1: One Voice. For this option, you need newsprint and a felt-tip pen (or a whiteboard and a dry-erase marker) and a blindfold.

Ask for one volunteer and have him come up to the front. Blindfold him and give him the marker. Explain that you are going to write down a word and the students are to guide the volunteer in drawing a picture of that word by yelling out instructions—but *not* telling the volunteer what the word is. Be sure to tell them that the louder, the better, so the instructions can be heard!

Once the volunteer is blindfolded, write the word "house" (remind the group not to say it out loud). At your signal, they should yell out instructions, such as "Draw a straight line across." Allow a few minutes to see how far the volunteer gets.

Let the volunteer see the results of his efforts, applaud his work and ask for another volunteer. Blindfold the new volunteer and give her the marker with the same instructions. The difference this time is that you will choose *only one student* to give the instructions to the volunteer. Write the word "car" and ask the instructor to begin giving directions. After a few minutes, remove the blindfold and congratulate both the instructor and the instructee on their fine piece of art!

Ask the first volunteer, "How did you feel when everyone was shouting directions at you?" (*Confused, frustrated, unsure.*) Ask the second volunteer, "How did you feel?" (*Guided, secure.*) Explain that we all need help in life, and friends are the perfect people to give us that help. Now, it might not be that we need friends to help us to do something like drawing, but we will probably need our friends around for more important things. The world is filled with all kinds of voices shouting different messages at us; it can be confusing and deafening. But when we need help and direction or maybe encouragement, the single voice of one friend can do the job.

Ask, "When are some times we need advice or help from a friend?" (*When we feel lonely; when we're having family problems; when we're struggling at school.*) "What are some things a good friend might say or ask that might be pretty tough to hear?" (*You really shouldn't be doing that; how's your relationship with God; you should tell your parents; you were wrong.*) Allow students to ponder this last question. Try to avoid hypothetical answers and push for real experiences when a friend dared to confront them.

Read Proverbs 12:15 and then explain, "The Bible tells us it's important to surround ourselves with friends who care enough to give good advice that will stretch us and challenge us even though it might hurt. This advice might even come from your youth leader. Ouch!"

Option 2: To Tell or Not to Tell? For this option, you need your Bible.

Introduce this step by explaining that just as Jonathan had David to tell him some harsh but important truths, we also need people in our lives who care enough to be brutally honest. Then read the following case study:

Katie and Natasha have been friends since the second grade, and best friends since the fifth. Now they are in seventh grade together. Their favorite topics of discussion these days are boys and clothes.

About two months into the school year, Katie begins to hear comments and criticisms from others about how Natasha wears "skimpy" clothes. She even hears some people call her derogatory names. Katie is hurt by what people are saying about her friend, but the harder thing is that she somewhat agrees with them. Natasha is dressing a little differently lately. She considers talking to her, but is too afraid Natasha will be hurt.

Katie loves Natasha, no matter what she wears. She just doesn't want her to get a reputation and really wants her to know what people are saying so maybe she can do something about it.

Ask the group if they would confront Natasha or not. If so, why? If they were in Katie's position, what would they say to Natasha? How might Natasha respond to Katie's confrontation?

Explain that there's a great verse in the Bible, Proverbs 12:15: "The way of a fool seems right to him, but a wise man listens to advice." God puts people in our lives to challenge, correct and confront us when we need it. If all we did with our friends was go to the mall and movies, we'd be poorer—both spiritually and financially! It's important that we allow friendships to develop to the place where we can ask hard questions and tell the truth even when it hurts.

APPLY

Option 1: Friend of Jesus. You'll need a lot of prayer and several gift Bibles to give to students who make a commitment to Christ during this session.

Explain that you've talked about friendships that help us grow, and that you're going to conclude by taking a closer look at the friendship that can help us grow more than any other. It's our friendship with Jesus. Read Mark 8:27-30 aloud, then explain that Jesus asked His friend Peter the most important question of all time: "Who do you say I am?" Explain that Jesus asks each of us that question, too: "Who do you say I am?" There are three ways to answer: Jesus is a liar, a lunatic or the Lord.

Tell the group that today, just like Peter, they have the chance to answer that question themselves. They might say that everything Jesus said and did was a lie, or they might say He was crazy. But if they believe He is their Lord, they need to acknowledge that fact. Ask them to repeat the following prayer after you:

Jesus (pause for students to repeat),
I know I often do wrong things (pause),
and I know I need You to be my Lord (pause).
Please come into my life (pause)
and take it over (pause). Amen.

Explain that if anyone prayed the prayer and intends to make Jesus the Lord of his or her whole life, the Bible teaches that all of heaven is rejoicing (see Luke 15:7)—and you want to rejoice with them! Ask any student who prayed with you to come and see you so that you can give them a Bible and answer any questions they might have about salvation.

Option 2: Growing-Up Questions. For this option, you will need copies of "Growing-Up Questions" (found on the next page) and pens or pencils.

Now that you've talked about our need to ask our friends some tough questions, explain that you want to get even more practical. Distribute copies of "Growing-Up Questions" and pens or pencils; then ask students to put a checkmark by each question they think they can ask someone important to them this week. (The handout questions correlate with varied levels of adolescent spiritual maturity, so there should be at least one question that will work for each student.)

After giving students a few minutes to do this, ask them to circle the *one* question they will commit to asking this week. Close in prayer, asking God to give each student the courage to approach a friend this week and ask him or her a question that will help him or her think and grow.

Youth Leader Tip

Approximately 60 percent of Christians say they accepted Jesus before the age of 18. This step allows them to make this important decision by describing the most important question that can help them grow: Who is Jesus?

GROWING-UP QUESTIONS

Check out these important people and put a check mark next to any question that you think you could ask them this week.

MY PARENTS

❏ What is one extra chore I can do this week to help you out?

❏ What is one thing you wish I understood about you?

❏ If everyone would drive the same speed, would all of the traffic jams on the highways disappear?

❏ What could I do to help us get along better at home?

MY GOD

❏ How do You want me to grow this week?

❏ Who do You want me to tell about You this week?

❏ How can I obey You when I'm around my friends?

❏ What's the square root of 9,586,342?

MY FRIENDS

❏ How can I help you with your homework this week?

❏ How can I be a better friend to you?

❏ Is there anything of mine you'd like to borrow?

❏ How do you get your hair so clean and shiny?

MY YOUTH LEADER

❏ Can I wash your car? Better yet, can I take up a collection to buy you a new car?

❏ How can I help out with the youth ministry this month?

❏ How can I be praying for you and your family?

REFLECT

The following short devotions are for the students to reflect on and answer during the week. You can make a copy of these pages and distribute to your class or print out from the PDF available online at **www.gospellight.com/un common/uncommon_jh_friends_and_peer_pressure.zip**.

1—SHARPEN UP

Flip to Proverbs 27:17 and get sharpened!

Imagine you're camping and it's time to roast some marshmallows. Oh, no! You forgot the wire coat hangers to put the marshmallows on! You find a nice long stick, but it has a blunt, thick tip. What could you rub it against to make it sharp?

- ❐   The lint in your pocket
- ❐   A piece of squishy gum stuck to your shoe
- ❐   A big hard rock
- ❐   The side of your nylon tent

Do you and your friends sharpen each other like iron sharpening iron, or are you squishy-soft like bubble gum?

_____
_____
_____
_____
_____
_____
_____

What do you think it means to be strong like iron?

_____
_____
_____
_____
_____
_____

What can you say that would help your friends to sharpen up today?

_____
_____
_____
_____
_____
_____
_____

2—SPEAK UP

Flip to Galatians 6:1-5 and see what you should be carrying for your friends.

Andrew and Jared were friends at church, but they didn't hang out that much together at school. It wasn't that they didn't like each other; they just hung out with different groups. Jared played on the school soccer team and spent most of his time with the kids on the team, and Andrew hung out with the skaters.

One day, Andrew stood a few people behind Jared in the lunch line and heard Jared and his friends making fun of the lunch lady, saying really mean things about her.

The next night at youth group, Andrew walked up to Jared when he was alone and said, "I heard what you were saying about Lunch Lady Lu Anne yesterday. I know you probably didn't mean to, but it sure didn't sound like stuff a Christian should be saying."

Sometimes your friends will tell you things that are hard to hear, and sometimes you'll have to tell your friends things that are hard to say. A friend might try to tell you a way you were sinning or you might feel God wants you to say something to one of your friends.

As you walk with God today, ask Him to help you listen to your friends and ask Him to give you the right words to say to them.

3—BUILD UP

Run, don't walk, to 1 Thessalonians 5:4-11 and learn how to build!

If you were going to build a fort for your little cousin in your backyard, what kind of things would you want to use to make the fort a strong one?

❐   A package of Pop Tarts, some straws and a jar of paste
❐   Two graham crackers, a gallon of paint and some peanut butter
❐   An old refrigerator box, some two-by-fours and a heavy blanket

Every conversation you have with your friends can build them and you, too. When you speak with your friends, are you giving them solid things, like encouragement and wisdom, to build with, or are the things you tell them silly or mean or sinful? Make it a point to be extra encouraging to all of your friends today.

4—MAN (OR WOMAN!) UP

Flip, flip, flip to Ruth 1:14-18 and read about an amazing friend.

Lydia was the most popular seventh grader at Flying Mongoose Junior High. She was the prettiest, most fun girl in the whole class and she made excellent brownies, too. Everyone liked her, especially her two good friends Angie and Cori and, of course, her boyfriend Jason, the most popular guy in the eighth grade.

In the summer before eighth grade, everything changed for Lydia. Her boyfriend dumped her, she got a really bad haircut, and to top it all off, she and her mom moved across town and she had to go to another school—Tiny Dog Middle School. Lydia told Cori and Angie that she didn't want them to hang out with her anymore. Cori said okay and went back to the friends she hung out with before she knew Lydia, but Angie said "No way!" and asked her parents to transfer her to Tiny Dog so Lydia wouldn't have to be alone.

Sometimes being a really good friend means doing things that may not be easy.

Is there a friend you know who is going through a tough time? Call him or her and ask how he or she is and if there is anything you can do to help.

If you're going through a hard time, call a friend and ask him or her to pray with you.

STRENGTHENING FRIENDSHIPS

THE BIG IDEA

Sharing true and honest feelings with each other strengthens our friendships.

SESSION AIMS

In this session you will guide students to (1) learn that friendships are strengthened through trust and honesty; (2) feel empowered to be honest in their close friendships; and (3) act by sharing at least one untold secret pain, fear or dream with one another.

THE BIGGEST VERSE

"And Jonathan had David reaffirm his oath out of love for him, because he loved him as he loved himself" (1 Samuel 20:17).

OTHER IMPORTANT VERSES

1 Samuel 20:5-17,41-42; Matthew 18:15-17; 1 Thessalonians 2:8

Note: Additional options and worksheets in 8¹/₂" x 11" format for this session are available for download at **www.gospellight.com/uncommon/jh_friends_and_peer_pressure.zip**.

STARTER

Option 1: Circle This. For this option, you need one copy of "Circle This" (found on the next page) for every two students, a whiteboard, a dry-erase marker and a blindfold. Ahead of time, cut the copies of "Circle This" into individual cards.

Greet students and explain that to start the session, you'll be assigning half of them to lie (they'll probably think, *Cool! It makes it legal when the youth leader asks us to do it!*) and half of them to tell the truth.

Next, choose one volunteer to come to the front. Give her the marker and blindfold her. Then distribute the cards to the remaining group and tell them not to blurt out what's on their cards. Half of them have the *false* diagram and half have the *true* diagram. (You decide which diagram is the true one and which is the false, but don't tell anyone.)

Instruct students to begin calling out instructions to the volunteer on how to draw the diagram that's on their card. The goal is to convince the volunteer that their diagram is the true one and to draw what's on their team's card. The key is for students to be very persuasive and strong in their coaching, trying to convince the volunteer that the other voices are lying.

Depending on the size of your particular group, the noise level in the room can be deafening as students begin to yell out instructions. The volunteer doing the drawing is not allowed to speak. Remind the volunteer that even his closest friend might hold a "false" card and to be very careful in deciding who to trust.

Give this a few minutes. When the volunteer is finished drawing, take off the blindfold and reveal the true card. Let the winning team revel in their victory and thank the volunteer.

Ask the volunteer, "Was it hard to trust the voices you heard? How did you know who to trust and who not to trust?" Let them share and allow the group to add any responses.

Explain that sometimes we feel like there are different voices telling us different things, just like our poor volunteer here. There's our mom, dad, teacher, sister, brother, friends, youth leader, even the TV! Who do we listen to? The bigger question is *who do we trust.* Friendships are strengthened when we share our real and honest feelings with each other. But in order to do that, we have to trust that person with our real and honest feelings.

Transition to the rest of the session by explaining that today you're going to look at how our friendships are strengthened by honest and deep sharing and how exercising the "muscle" of trust can help us do that.

CIRCLE THIS

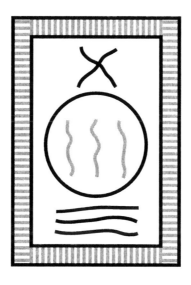

Option 2: Trust Walk. For this option, you need blindfolds for half of the group members. Ahead of time, plot a course for a Trust Walk, perhaps starting in the meeting room and ending at the front door of the church.

Greet students and explain that today they're going to do a Trust Walk through the church building. Explain that although they may have done it before, it's time to exercise their trust muscles again. Invite them to pair up and give them a blindfold.

Blindfold the tallest person on each team and instruct students that in this Trust Walk, no touching is allowed. The teams have 10 minutes to complete the course and the walk is done by voice instruction only. When each team reaches the turn-around point (the front door of the church), the teams should switch roles to come back to the meeting room.

Reward the team that finishes first with cheers, applause and a standing ovation, then transition to the next step by explaining that trust is a big part of friendships. Today, you're going to discover how it goes hand in hand with sharing our honest and deepest feelings.

MESSAGE

Option 1: Characteristics of Friendship. For this option, you need several Bibles, poster board (or construction paper) and markers. Ahead of time, cut the poster board or construction paper into eight 12x18-inch sheets. Write the following characteristics, each on a different sheet, in large print: "Loyalty," "Trust," "Love," "Commitment," "Faithfulness," "Communication," "Respect" and "Kindness."

Ask nine volunteers to come forward and give eight of them one sign each. Have the sign holders line up in random order facing the rest of the group. Instruct the rest of the group to work together to come up with a consensus regarding the order of importance of the characteristics when it comes to developing close friendships. The ninth volunteer is "Vanna White" and

Youth Leader Tip

Students may disagree and challenge each other's thinking during this exercise, and that's okay. However, you may need to facilitate the discussion if they are struggling to come up with a majority vote.

moves the cardholders into their new places. Try picking on the guys in the group to play this role just for fun!

When the group has finished arranging, have the sign holders sit down where they are, holding their signs in front of them. Invite the rest of the group to open their Bibles to 1 Samuel 20 and explain that you're going to read 1 Samuel 20:5-17,41-42 to search for these characteristics in David and Jonathan's friendship.[1] Ask volunteers to read one verse each, and as they come to the verses where a characteristic shows up (see below), stop and ask the group: *Which of the words is displayed in that verse?* As they identify the characteristics in David and Jonathan's friendship, invite the person holding that card to stand and move back.

- Kindness (vv. 5-8a)
- Commitment (v. 8b)
- Loyalty (v. 9)
- Communication (vv. 10-13)

- Faithfulness (vv. 14-15)
- Love (vv. 16-17)
- Respect (v. 41)
- Trust (v. 42)

Once all the words have been identified, continue: David and Jonathan shared some hard times together. In those hard times they grew to trust each other with their honest thoughts and feelings. The more they trusted, the more they shared; and the more they shared, the stronger their friendship became. Evidence of this is found in verse 17: "And Jonathan had David reaffirm his oath out of love for him, because he loved him as he loved himself."

Transition to the next step by explaining that just like David and Jonathan, our friendships can be strengthened by trusting someone enough to share our honest thoughts and real feelings with them.

Option 2: Trust, Honesty and Sharing. For this option, you need several Bibles, a whiteboard and a dry-erase marker.

Ask students, "When you hear the words 'best friends,' which two best friends at your school come to mind?" Let them throw out some answers, which will likely be the names of two girls. If so, make mention of it and ask, "Isn't it interesting that the model of friendship in the Bible is the friendship between two men?" Point out that girls and guys do some things differently in friendships, but there are three things common in all close friendships: trust, honesty and sharing.

Write the words "trust," "honesty" and "sharing" on the whiteboard. Explain to students that they should listen carefully as you read the Scripture passage and shout out one of those words as it applies to the story. Some may yell out two different words at the same time. That's okay, because that means they're listening! Read 1 Samuel 20:5-17,41-42. If they need help, you might want to pause while reading the verses and wait.

Explain that the deeper David and Jonathan shared, the deeper their friendship grew. These guys didn't just share what they did last weekend and talk about who won the chariot championships. They dug deep and risked big. They were honest and real.

As the division between David and Jonathan's father grew wider, Jonathan and David's friendship grew stronger. Sometimes it takes a crisis to bring two people closer. But we don't have to wait for one for it to happen!

DIG

Option 1: Pointers for Pete. For this option, you need several Bibles, copies of "Pointers for Pete" (found on the next page) and pens or pencils. Read the following case study aloud:

> Pete is in the seventh grade and a pretty average student. He goes to church and accepted Jesus as Savior when he was five years old, but last summer he made a solid decision to live for God and has tried to hang out with the right kind of friends who will have a positive influence on him.
>
> Although he has good Christian friends, there is no one that Pete shares his deepest, most honest feelings with. His parents are great but they're, well, parents. Lately he has been struggling with feeling pretty unimportant and insignificant, especially in light of all of the athletic types and heartthrobs at his school. He's been noticing girls a lot more lately and is finding he's scared to death of them! These thoughts and feelings make him feel depressed.
>
> There are a couple of guys from the youth group that Pete hangs out with, but he hasn't been able to share with them what's going on inside. He can probably talk to his youth pastor, but he really wishes he could talk to someone his own age, like maybe Jason. Jason is always nice to him and often asks how things are going. Pete gives the safe answer, "Great!" He just wishes he could say the truth: *I'm feeling really bummed, a little lonely and will probably never, ever date in my life.* But he doesn't.

POINTERS FOR PETE

Use David and Jonathan's friendship in 1 Samuel 20 as a model of trust and sharing as you give Pete advice. You can only give advice that you are willing to practice yourself!

Hey, Pete!

I know you're struggling with sharing your thoughts and feelings with friends. I'd like to give you some pointers:

Always . . .

_____
_____
_____
_____
_____
_____

Never . . .

_____
_____
_____
_____
_____

Remember to Be . . .

_____
_____
_____
_____
_____
_____
_____

Distribute pens or pencils and "Pointers for Pete" and explain that each student is appointed to give Pete three pointers for sharing his feelings and deepening his friendships. The three pointers need to start with "Always," "Never" and "Be." They should use David and Jonathan's friendship in 1 Samuel 20 as a model of trust and sharing as they give Pete advice.

Here's the catch: They can only give advice that they are willing to practice themselves!

Allow students to work in pairs and give them five minutes to write their "Pointers for Pete." Have several pairs share their answers. Praise and commend them on their great advice.

Option 2: *The Horse Whisperer.* For this option, you need a TV, a DVD player and the movie *The Horse Whisperer.*

Ahead of time, cue the DVD approximately one hour and 45 minutes from beginning to the scene in which the daughter runs to her room, slams the door and sulks on her bed. When her mom tries to talk to her, she clams up and pouts. Just when her mom gives up and turns to leave, she begins to cry and starts to let it all out. A touching moment!

Note: Parts of this film may be inappropriate for a junior-high audience (even though many students may have seen the movie, there may be some parents who do not allow such viewing), so you and your senior pastor and the parents will be better friends afterward if you cue the movie to the right scene.

Introduce the clip by explaining that in this movie, a young girl is in a riding accident and she ends up losing one of her legs. Her anger causes her to go into a shell and her already strained relationship with her mother is now void of any closeness or conversation. Finally, one night it all comes out. Grab the Kleenex!

After the clip, explain that although this particular scene is being played out between a daughter and a mother, this situation can relate to friendships as well.

Youth Leader Tip

Students are taking a risk during this exercise by revealing their thoughts and feelings before their peers. Don't underestimate their potential for depth, honesty and vulnerability, and lead the way by sharing your own personal story.

Next, discuss the following:

- Why do you think it was so hard for the daughter to open up and share her real feelings? *She was embarrassed, afraid, hurt, proud.*
- How do you think she felt after she shared what was really bothering her? *Relieved, safe, closer to her mom.*
- Could anyone in the group share about a time when you risked telling someone your deepest and most honest feelings and were glad you did? What happened?

APPLY

Option 1: Do You Know? For this option, you need copies of "Do You Know?" (found on the next page) and pens or pencils.

Introduce this step by explaining that right now you're going to give students an opportunity to practice what you've been talking about—honestly sharing our thoughts and feelings with one another.

Distribute pens or pencils and "Do You Know?" and give students several minutes to complete the statements.

Next, divide students into groups of two or three and instruct them to share their answers with each other. After a few minutes, close the session by praying that God will give boldness and courage to students to share what they are thinking and feeling with their friends.

Option 2: Friendship Bracelets. For this option, you need a package or spool of leather rope, embroidery floss, yarn, macramé string or any other suitable "friendship bracelet" material.

Explain to students that you want to close by looking at how easily this session on sharing in friendships can be applied during the next week. Encourage them to go deeper by sharing a secret ouch—a pain or disappointment they've kept inside—to someone within the next seven days.

Give each student a piece of leather, approximately eight inches long. If they decide to take the risk, explain to them, "After you've shared with your friend, ask them if they will tie the leather on your wrist as a sign that you shared." (*Note:* Next week when you meet, make sure to ask who's got the bracelet on!)

Close by praying that God would give the students courage to share true and honest feelings with their close friends.

Do You Know?

If I could live with anyone I wanted to, I would live with . . .

_____
_____
_____
_____

If I could live anywhere in the world, I would live . . .

_____
_____
_____
_____

My dream in life is to . . .

_____
_____
_____
_____

My biggest fear is . . .

_____
_____
_____
_____

If I had all the money I wanted, I would . . .

_____
_____
_____

A goal I have for this year is . . .

_____
_____
_____
_____

REFLECT

The following short devotions are for the students to reflect on and answer during the week. You can make a copy of these pages and distribute to your class or print out from the PDF available online at **www.gospellight.com/un common/uncommon_jh_friends_and_peer_pressure.zip.**

1—FRIENDLY FEEDBACK

Find Proverbs 24:26 and listen up!

Imagine for a moment that you have to write a really important paper for your English class; in fact, your teacher tells you that it will count for half of your grade! The topic is hard and you work on it for a long, long time. When you are done, you ask some people what they think of it. Whose opinion would you listen to the most?

❏ Your Grandma: "It's nice, dear . . . and what pretty paper you printed it on!"

❏ Your brother: "Yeah, it's a good paper . . . by the way, can I borrow 10 bucks?"

❏ Your best friend: "It's all right, but you need a stronger introduction and you had a few errors in grammar. Do you want me to help you with it?"

❏ Your Mom and Dad: "Well, I didn't really have time to read it, but I skimmed it. It looked fine to me."

Can you depend on your friends to tell you the truth, even when the news is not good?

_____

_____

_____

_____

_____

_____

_____

Are you a friend that is honest, even when you have to tell your friend something he or she may not want to hear?

_____

_____

_____

_____

_____

_____

Pray that God will help you to be an honest friend today.

2—HONESTLY!

Leap into John 8:32 and see how to get free!

John and Jake both tried out for the football team. Both made the first and second cuts, but at the final tryout, they were both told that they didn't make the team.

John was so upset that he told his friends, "There was no way I could have made that team. The coach didn't like me from the beginning, and all the other guys trying out cheated. Man, I'm so mad, this is so unfair!"

Jake was really upset too, but he told his friends, "I just wasn't good enough, I guess. I really wanted to be on the team, but I'll just have to work out more and try out again next year."

It's important to be honest with your friends and with yourself. What John told his friends just covered up the fact that he was hurt, but Jake's friends were able to know how he really felt, and because of that, they became better friends.

Do you tell your friends the truth about yourself, even when you are hurt or scared or sad?

_____

_____

_____

_____

_____

_____

What is one thing that is making you feel hurt or scared or sad that you could tell a friend about today?

_____

_____

_____

_____

_____

_____

3—STRETCHING THE TRUTH

Read Hebrews 3:12-15 and decide if you're hard or soft!
Have you ever stretched the truth and said something to your friends like:

- ❏ "Oh, I've met Zac Efron" when really you just saw the back of his head at the airport, from a distance?
- ❏ "I totally know how to drive" when you only know how to drive a golf cart?
- ❏ "I've been to so many concerts I can't even count" when you've only been to two?
- ❏ "I love horror movies. They're so cool" when the only one you've seen gave you nightmares?

Sometimes it's hard just to be yourself around your friends. Although sometimes stretching the truth seems to be the key to getting people to like you, it isn't the best way to treat your friends. Honesty is a two-way street, and if you want to believe what your friends tell you, you need to be honest with them. Promise yourself and God that you will be truthful with your friends this week.

4—WHO TO TRUST?

Read Proverbs 27:6 and see what you can trust!
Linda and Karry went shopping together, looking for just the right outfit for the school dance the next Friday. While looking in the mirror after trying on a dress, Linda saw Leana and Trina behind her, the two most popular—and the meanest—girls in school. They *oohed* and *ahhed* about the dress and told her

how she had to buy it and wear it to the dance. Leana and Trina had never even spoken to her before, and Linda was so impressed, she bought the dress without asking Karry what she thought.

Later, Karry said, "Are you sure about that dress? It didn't fit very well and I don't think the color is very good," but Linda thought Leana and Trina knew better than Karry. When she wore the dress to the dance, Leana and Trina came up to her and said very loudly, "I can't believe what you're wearing. That's the ugliest thing I've ever seen!"—and they both walked away laughing.

Sometimes we forget that our friends are really on our side, especially when they tell us something we don't want to hear. Who do you listen to, your friends or the crowd? Why?

_____

_____

_____

_____

_____

_____

Who is one friend you can count on to tell you the truth? In what ways can you count on that friend?

_____

_____

_____

_____

_____

_____

Today, be sure to thank God for that special friend. And also thank him or her for being such a good friend.

SERVING OUR FRIENDS

THE BIG IDEA

Taking risks to serve each other deepens our friendships.

SESSION AIMS

In this session you will guide students to (1) discover that it is important to God that we serve others; (2) feel the personal satisfaction that comes from giving and helping others; and (3) act by identifying one way to serve their friends this week.

THE BIGGEST VERSE

"Jonathan got up from the table in fierce anger; on that second day of the month he did not eat, because he was grieved at his father's shameful treatment of David" (1 Samuel 20:34).

OTHER IMPORTANT VERSES

1 Samuel 20:24-42; Matthew 5–7; Mark 3:1-6; Luke 10:30-37; John 13:35; Romans 12:10; Philippians 2:3-4; James 2:14

Note: Additional options and worksheets in 8$^1/_2$" x 11" format for this session are available for download at **www.gospellight.com/uncommon/jh_friends_and_peer_pressure.zip**.

STARTER

Option 1: Objects of Service. For this option, you need a brown paper bag containing 5 to 10 items (such as a coffee mug, a pen and pencil set, or a hair accessory) purchased from a dollar store or picked up from your home or office. *Note:* You will be giving away these items, so if they are from your home or office, make sure you don't want or need them anymore!

Greet students and explain that today you're going to look at what it means to serve others. Then give these instructions: "I'm going to give this bag to one of you and I want that person to reach into the bag and pull out something. Once you pull an item out of the bag, you need to quickly yell out a way to use that object to serve someone. There's a catch, though. Before I give you the bag, I'm going to name someone (for instance, your science teacher, your mom, your dad, your neighbor, the person who sits next to you in English) and that person is the one your object must serve! If someone else yells out a way it can be used to serve that person before you do, they get to keep it."

Repeat this several times by giving the bag to several different students, until the bag is empty. Transition to the next step by explaining that now you're going to look at how serving, giving and helping are important steps in making friendships strong and lasting. So important, by the way, that the Bible talks a lot about them.

Option 2: The Big Giveaway. For this option, you need 10 pennies for each person present and a bag of miniature chocolate bars.

As students arrive, give each one 10 pennies. Introduce this new session by explaining that the session focuses on serving and giving to each other in our friendships . . . and you're going to start by actually giving to each other right now.

Explain that students have approximately 60 seconds to give away as many pennies as you can. There are only two rules: (1) If someone offers them

Youth Leader Tip

One the quickest and easiest steps students can take to reach out to their friends is to invite them to church. Your job as a youth leader is to make sure visitors feel welcome and understand what is happening.

a penny they must take it, and (2) they can only give away one penny at a time. On your mark, get set, go!

After 60 seconds, call the group back from chaos and ask who has the least amount of pennies. Congratulate the winner(s) for being so giving. If there is more than one winner, give each one a piece of candy—if there's only one winner, give him or her the whole bag! Collect the pennies and show your own giving spirit by donating them to the missionary fund.

Ask students how it felt to give and how it felt to receive. Allow for responses, then transition to the next step by explaining, "Let's look at what God says about giving, serving and helping our friends."

MESSAGE

Option 1: The Saga of the Good Samaritan. For this option, you need your Bible, a roll of toilet paper, a rolled-up newspaper, three hats (the funkier the better), a small pillow or cushion, an overshirt, a backpack and one copy of "The Saga of the Good Samaritan" (found on the next page). Ahead of time, practice reading the script at least twice so you can read it smoothly in front of the students.

Remind students that they've been studying David and Jonathan's friendship as a great example from the Old Testament of friendship. Designate a "group Bible for the day" (either your own or one of your students') and pass it around, asking students to read aloud one to three verses from 1 Samuel 20:24-42 until the passage is finished. Once it is finished, ask, "What kind of risks did David and Jonathan take to serve each other?"

Explain that it's not just in the Old Testament that we learn about friendships, but also in the New Testament. Jesus Himself told a great story about friendship in Luke 10:30-37 that you're going to look at together.

Ask for nine volunteers to act in a fun dramatization of Luke 10:30-37. Assign the actors their roles, give them the appropriate props and ask them to step to the side.

The instructions are simple: They should repeat what you say and do what you tell them using what you gave them. (*Note:* The words listed in quotation marks should be repeated. The words in bold type are the narration. Whenever you see the word "pause" or other directions in parentheses, that means that you should pause to let the stduents say their lines or do the action. Read the skit with dramatic inflection and lots of volume.) So begins the saga of "The Good Samaritan."

The Saga of the Good Samaritan

The Cast and Props

A bad man holding a rolled-up newspaper
A thief holding a pillow
A robber missing one shoe
A Pharisee wearing a hat
A priest wearing a hat and carrying a Bible
The Good Samaritan carrying a roll of toilet paper in a backpack
An innkeeper wearing the funkiest hat
A certain man (wearing a T-shirt and a loose overshirt)
A donkey (no prop, just a strong back!)

The Narration

One day a certain man was walking down the road, whistling as he went (pause), when all of a sudden, a thief, a bad man and a robber jumped out (pause while thief, bad man and robber enter) and attacked the certain man.

They hit him (pause), and kicked him (pause), and when he fell to the ground they kicked him and hit him some more (pause).

They took all of his money and they stole his clothes right off his back (pause)! And then they ran off like the cowards that they were, laughing like a band of hyenas. (Pause—if they don't laugh, repeat, "laughing like a band of hyenas.") And the certain man lay there in the road and moaned (cue him to moan painfully) and groaned (groan) in pain and agony. (Cue him to say "pain and agony!")

Down the same road a priest came along, praying as he went, "Oh God, bless me today." (Pause.) He came upon the certain man who moaned (pause for the moan) and groaned (pause for the groan) in pain and agony (pause—"pain and agony").

The priest said, "Why, look! A certain man." (Pause.) And he gently kicked him to see if he was still alive. And the man moaned (moan) and groaned (groan) in pain and agony ("pain and agony"). "He looks like he needs help," said the priest (pause). "I should pray for him" (pause).

Then he looked at his watch and gasped, "But not right now! I'll be late for church!" (pause). And he went on his way. And the certain man moaned and groaned in pain and agony (more moaning and groaning—the certain man should have it down by now!).

Next, a Pharisee came down the same road humming a happy tune (pause), but his nose was so far in the air, he almost tripped over the certain man lying there (pause). And the certain man moaned . . . and groaned . . . in pain and agony. (By this time, your tone is a bit "yadda, yadda, hurry it up" when it comes to the moan, groan, pain and agony part.)

The Pharisee said, "Why, look! A certain man!" (Pause.) He was disgusted and said, "He shouldn't be lying in the road like this! He's naked!" (Pause.) And the Pharisee stepped over the certain man and went on his way. And the certain man moaned . . . and groaned . . . in pain and agony (pause).

Just then, the Good Samaritan came walking down the same road with his donkey by his side. (Pause.) He saw the naked certain man and yelled, "Oh, no! A poor, bleeding, naked, certain man!" (Pause.) The terrible thief, bad man and robber must have done this!" (Pause.)

In the distance, he could hear the terrible thief, bad man and robber laughing like hyenas. (Laughing in the background.)

The Good Samaritan knelt down and took bandages (the toilet paper roll) from his pack. He began to bandage the certain man's head. (Allow Good Sam to roll a good amount of toilet paper layers around the certain man's head.) Then the Good Samaritan picked up the certain man (pause) and put him on his donkey (pause).

And the certain man moaned (moan) and groaned (groan) in pain and agony. (Sound even more rushed as you wait for the moans, groans and pain and agonies.) He took the certain man to an inn and said to the innkeeper (appearing on the scene), "Here is some money. Please take care of him while I'm gone (pause). If he runs up a higher bill, I'll pay it when I get back." (Pause.)

And the Good Samaritan paid the innkeeper to take care of the certain man and went on his way (pause). And that was the last we heard of the (here we go again!) moans and groans and the pain and agony.

The end.

After the drama is over, call all of the actors back up for a much-deserved standing ovation. If you have time, call them up separately and let them take a bow.

Explain that this story—*slightly* edited—is taken from Luke 10. Show the students in your group an open Bible turned to Luke 10 and tell them that Jesus used the story as an example of helping others even when it's not the popular thing to do. It was a risk for the Samaritan to stop and help a Jew who was stranded and wounded along the road. The same guys who attacked the man could have attacked him, but he chose to take the chance and help out. Then Jesus said in verse 37 to His original listeners as well as to us today: "Go and do likewise."

Transition to the next step by asking, "Have you ever taken a risk to help a friend or someone who is not a friend? Think about it as we move on to the next step."

Option 2: *Forrest Gump*. For this option, you will need several Bibles, a TV, a DVD player and a copy of *Forrest Gump*. Ahead of time, cue the video approximately 53 minutes from the beginning to the scene in which Forrest is trying to find his "best, good friend Bubba" in the midst of a battle in the Vietnam War. Watch this clip ahead of time to make sure you avoid any controversial language.

Note: Other parts of this video would be inappropriate for a junior-high audience (even though many students may have seen the movie, there may be some whose parents do not allow such viewing), so you and your senior pastor and the parents will be better friends afterward if you cue the film to the right scene.

Set up the movie clip by explaining that Forrest Gump was a rather simple man who had a "best, good friend," Bubba. They met while they were serving in the military together. One day while the two are walking through a jungle with the rest of their patrol, they are attacked. Forrest is unharmed and he desperately tries to find Bubba and save him. Then play the clip.

After playing the clip, ask, "Why did Forrest go back and risk his own life to find Bubba? What do you think Forrest felt when he finally found him?"

Give an overview to 1 Samuel 20:24-42 by explaining that just like Forrest and Bubba, Jonathan covered David's back. David's life was in danger and Jonathan helped him escape. Jonathan risked not only ruining the relationship between him and his father in order to help out his friend, but also being killed or injured.

Invite students to read the story in 1 Samuel 20:24-42 for themselves. Explain that friendship can be risky business when we really care about someone. David and Jonathan were so committed to each other that each would risk his life to help the other.

Ask the students what risks they have taken to help a friend. What risks have they seen others take to help a friend? Transition to the next step by explaining that serving others strengthens our friendships and lets people know we care. Jesus did the same thing for us by giving His very life! This serving thing is a big deal to God!

DIG

Option 1: If I Were a Tree. For this option, you need copies of "If I Were a Tree . . ." (found on the next page), pens or pencils, and the book *The Giving Tree* by Shel Silverstein. This book is available in most secular bookstores, and once you get it, you'll be glad you have it.

Read *The Giving Tree* to students. If the group is small enough, make sure you hold the book so that students can see each picture. When the story is finished, discuss the following:

- When was the tree happiest? *After she gave to the boy.*
- If you were the tree, how would you feel after you gave and gave? *Used, unappreciated; like I was wasting my time;* or maybe *good, useful, satisfied, happy.*
- How is the Giving Tree like Jesus? *Jesus sacrificed Himself and gave of Himself for us.*

Distribute pens or pencils and "If I Were a Tree . . ." and explain that it's easy to feel good about giving when we get something back in return or when someone else notices. But the true test of friendship is giving even when

Youth Leader Tip

In every situation, junior-highers need to know that Jesus is "Immanuel: God with us." Remind them that Jesus is ready to meet them where they are right now, promising them: "I'll stick with you—forever."[1]

IF I WERE A TREE . . .

Imagine you were the tree in the story *The Giving Tree*. In each of these descriptions, you'll see what the tree did and what you could do for your friends that would be similar. Don't worry! We're not expecting you to grow any apples or branches. Write the name of a friend that you could give each gift. You can list the same friend more than once.

Play under my shade and swing from my branches.

I would invite _____ to do this because he/she needs something fun and uplifting right now.

Take my apples and sell them.

I would offer this to _____ because he/she could use the extra help.

Take my branches and build a house.

I would give this to _____ because things aren't so great in his/her house lately.

Take my trunk and build a boat to sail away.

I would offer this to _____ because life's a little hard for him/her right now and he/she needs a break.

Sit down on my tree stump and rest.

I would offer this to _____ because he's/she's a little beat up lately and he/she needs a rest.

Note
Adapted from Shel Silverstein, *The Giving Tree* (New York: Harper & Row, 1964).

it is difficult or hurts and even when no one notices. Give students a minute or two to complete the handout, and then have them pray silently for each friend they've listed.

Option 2: Sacrifice. For this option, you need nothing but this book!
Read the following illustration:

Katie and Lisa have been friends for a long time. They go to the same church and this year they're in the same eighth-grade homeroom together. Lisa is an above-average student, but Katie has always struggled with her grades and has to work at them twice as long and hard as Lisa does.

Next Friday is a school party and both girls have been looking forward to going for weeks. They plan to go together with a few other friends. Lisa has a crush on Jerome, and a few of her friends told her they heard him say that if he sees Lisa at the party, he'll ask her to dance with him. She's so excited and can't wait to go.

The day before the party, Katie calls Lisa in tears. Her parents have grounded her from the party because of her low grades. She has to spend the weekend studying for a math test on Monday. After about 10 minutes of "Oh my gosh! I can't believe this! I hate my parents," Lisa and Katie hang up.

As Lisa lies on her bed, she can't help thinking of her friend and her pain. Not only is Katie hurting, but she's also struggling with her math work. Math comes easy for Lisa and she's all ready for Mr. Ward's math test on Monday. She realizes that if she spends the weekend with Katie to help her study, it would make a big difference in Katie's grade, and they might be able to salvage part of the weekend and do something fun together. But she doesn't want to miss the party either. This could be the big night for her and Jerome. Should she risk the chance and help her friend?

Discuss the following:

- If you were Lisa, what would you do? If you were Katie, what would you tell Lisa to do?
- How would you feel if you were Katie and your friend chose to go to the party without you?

- How would you feel if your friend chose to help you study instead of going to the party?

Explain that developing important friendships can sometimes bring difficult choices to those involved, but our willingness to make choices to meet
our friends' needs over our own wants and desires will build strong founda-
tions for our friendships.

APPLY

Option 1: If You Ever Need a Hand. For this option, you need a copy machine
close by, copies of "If You Ever Need a Hand . . ." (found on the next page), and
pens or pencils. Ahead of time, practice photocopying your handprint onto the
handout so that the image comes out in the middle of the page.

Tell students that you're all going on a little field trip to the church office.
When you get there, place copies of "If You Ever Need a Hand . . ." in the paper supply tray. Invite each student to place one hand, palm down, on the copy
machine, close the lid and make a copy of each person's hand.

When everyone has a copy of their hand, head back to the youth room.
Distribute pens or pencils and ask students to sign their names on their own
page, fold it in half and write down the name of the person they want to give
it to. Encourage them to deliver the paper by the end of the day tomorrow.

Close by praying that God will help students meet the needs of others.

Option 2: The "Help" Button. For this option, you need one button of any
kind for each student.

Ask students to think about a computer. In almost every kind of software,
there's a button you can click if you get stuck and need some answers. What's
that button called? The "Help" button. When we work on the computer, we
sometimes get stuck and need help. And sometimes we also need help in real
life. Challenge students to be that "Help" button for their friends this week
when they're feeling stuck, hurt, lonely or troubled.

Distribute the buttons, one for each person. Invite students to take the button and keep it in their pockets all week as a reminder to serve their friends.
Then, at the end of the week, they should pass the "Help" button on to someone else, pledging their friendship and challenging them to be someone else's
"Help" button. Spend time in prayer asking students to pray for their friends by
name and for God's help to serve them.

If You Ever Need a Hand . . .

You Can Count on Mine!

"Each of you should look not only to your own interests, but also to the interests of others."

P HILIPPIANS 2:4

REFLECT

The following short devotions are for the students to reflect on and answer during the week. You can make a copy of these pages and distribute to your class or print out from the PDF available online at **www.gospellight.com/un common/uncommon_jh_friends_and_peer_pressure.zip.**

1—WHAT IF . . . ?

Hey! Go read John 15:12-13 right now!
What if your friend asked you to:

- Give up your favorite sport to tutor him/her in math?
- Use your allowance to buy him/her a pizza?
- Spend the weekend helping him or her move instead of going to the beach?
- Take care of his or her bratty little brother while he or she went to a dance?

What would you do if your best friend asked you to die so he or she could live?

_____

_____

_____

_____

_____

_____

Jesus loved you so much He gave up His life for you—His friend. What do you do for your friends? Do you ever sacrifice your time, money or your comfort to serve them? Why or why not?

_____

_____

_____

_____

_____

_____

_____

Find a way to serve a friend today, like helping him/her to clean his/her room or do his/her chores or taking him/her to a movie.

2—SERVING YOUR CHURCH FAMILY

Do you want to know what to do? Read Galatians 5:13 and find out!

At church, Nina and Carrie liked to goof off. They made fun of the younger kids, didn't sing during worship, talked during the sermon and giggled, and poked each other whenever a leader tried to get them to behave. They thought that, because they were Christians, they could do anything they wanted to other Christians.

Ellen and Lucy loved their church and liked to help out, but Nina and Carrie really distracted them. Ellen and Lucy asked Nina and Carrie to please be quiet and respectful in church, but they only got worse. Why did Nina and Carrie treat Ellen and Lucy as if they didn't really matter?

At church and with your Christian friends, sometimes it's easy to sit back and be served by others, never giving back. It's important to remember that being a Christian means giving to other Christians. Pray for your church today and ask God to show you a way you can serve there.

3—SMELLY FEET

Look up John 13:1-5 and look down at your feet. When was the last time you washed those things?

Do you think you could do it if your best friend in the whole world asked you to:

- Wash his/her dog, Mr. Stinky?
- Sell all your things and give him/her the money?
- Clean his/her filthy bedroom?
- Run a 400-mile race with no shoes on?
- Clean his/her toilet with your favorite T-shirt?

When Jesus got down and washed His disciples' feet, they were totally amazed because in those days, washing other people's feet was about as cool as washing gas-station toilets with your own toothbrush! Can you think of some totally amazing way you could serve your friends this week?

_____

_____

_____

_____

_____

_____

4—SHARING EVERYTHING

Flip to Philemon 6-7. Can you find it with your eyes closed?

Kelly and Mike were friends from school. Every day they would eat lunch together, and Mike would make Kelly laugh by making milk come out of his nose, and Kelly would make Mike laugh by throwing Jell-O squares in the air and catching them in her mouth. After school they would walk home to- gether, kicking the pebbles in the road and telling each other jokes. Some- times they would hang out on Saturdays, but every Sunday Kelly went to church. Mike had never gone to church and wondered what it was all about, but Kelly never invited him.

The best thing you could ever do for a friend is show him or her the way to Christ.

Who are your non-Christian friends? Write their names down somewhere that you will see them every day and pray for them. Invite them to church, pray for your meals in front of them and let them know how in love with Je- sus you are!

GOSSIP

THE BIG IDEA

Gossip can wreck and ruin friendships.

SESSION AIMS

In this session you will guide students to (1) discover how words can damage their relationships; (2) see the importance of putting an end to damaging conversation; and (3) act by speaking kindly about their friends.

THE BIGGEST VERSE

"Saul said to them, 'Listen, men of Benjamin! Will the son of Jesse give all of you fields and vineyards? Will he make all of you commanders of thousands and commanders of hundreds? Is that why you have all conspired against me? No one tells me when my son makes a covenant with the son of Jesse. None of you is concerned about me or tells me that my son has incited my servant to lie in wait for me, as he does today!'" (1 Samuel 22:7-8).

OTHER IMPORTANT VERSES

1 Samuel 22:6-8; Psalm 12:1-8; Matthew 5:23-24; 6:14; Colossians 3:8-9,12-14; 4:5; James 1:26; 3:5-6; 1 Peter 3:10

Note: Additional options and worksheets in $8^1/_2$" x 11" format for this session are available for download at **www.gospellight.com/uncommon/jh_friends_and_peer_pressure.zip**.

STARTER

Option 1: Curiously Strong. For this option, you need a tin of Altoids "curiously strong" mints—extra-strong would be even better.

Greet the group and pass around the Altoids mints and invite everyone to take one and place it in their mouths, not because they need them, but to make a point. Some students might begin to make mention of how strong they are. Challenge them to try to keep the mint in one place in their mouth for as long as possible. It should be hard to do!

How can such a tiny thing be so powerful?! That's the claim to fame of Altoids. Explain that today, you're going to talk about something else that is very small, yet very powerful. It's something we all have; in fact, it's in your mouth, right along with your mint! That's right, your tongue.

Read James 3:5 and then ask the group, "How can such a little muscle as the tongue cause such great pain? Let's explore today, especially now that we all have fresh breath."

Option 2: Tricky Telephone. For this option, you need nothing but the tongue-twisters listed below.

Greet the students and introduce the new session by explaining that today, you're going to focus on something very small but very powerful. Divide the students into groups of 8 to 10 people each and have them sit on the floor in a circle with their legs crossed. (If you have a small group, just make one circle.)

Tell students that you're going to whisper something in the ear of one person in each circle, then that person will whisper the information to the person on his left, and the message must get passed around from ear to ear until it reaches the person who started it. Remind students that each person is only allowed to whisper the message one time, so they must listen carefully! And *whisper!*

In each group, whisper one of the following statements to the person who comes the closest to touching their tongue to their nose (if you need more than three statements, just use the same ones more than once).

- They say that if a baby learns to walk early, it will probably not learn to talk early, and if it learns to talk early, it'll probably walk later.
- Psychologists say that the normal person can have as many as 700 chances to speak every day and that a talkative person can use as many as 100,000 words in a day.

- It's a known fact that girls talk more than guys, but the jury is still out on whether or not it's related to brain activity levels.

When everyone is finished, have the last person in each group report the statement he/she ended up with; then read the original message you gave to each group. You should have quite a discrepancy!

Explain that this is exactly how gossip works: As it gets passed from person to person, it can get distorted, confused and downright untrue. Most of the time, it isn't something anyone else is supposed to know about in the first place! And it all begins with one little thing: the tongue. Today you're going to study this small but powerful thing that is able to cause both damage and pain in a single bound.

MESSAGE

Option 1: King Saul's Voice. For this option, you need a cardboard crown (available at most party supply stores or get one free from your local Burger King restaurant).

Invite two volunteers to come to the front of the room. Explain that they will be doing a scene from the Bible, but King Saul's throat is pretty sore from yelling all day, so he will need a voice double for this scene. One volunteer will play King Saul, wearing the crown, and the other will be the voice double. The voice double should stand directly behind the king and try very hard not to be seen.

Instruct the voice double to read 1 Samuel 22:7-8 slow enough so that King Saul can move his mouth as the words are spoken. King Saul should animate the scene by moving his hands and arms and use overacted facial expressions. If this is done correctly, it should come out looking like the worst-dubbed martial arts movie ever.

Youth Leader Tip

Studies have shown that while nearly one in three teenagers attend a youth group every week, half of the attendees are not born-again Christians. You have the chance to be an evangelist—to share the good news of Christ with them—on a regular basis.[1]

Begin by narrating verse 6: "Now Saul heard that David and his men had been discovered. And Saul, spear in hand, was seated under the tamarisk tree on the hill at Gibeah, with all his officials standing around him."

The voice double should then read verses 7 and 8: "Listen, men of Benjamin! Will the son of Jesse give all of you fields and vineyards? Will he make all of you commanders of thousands and commanders of hundreds? Is that why you have all conspired against me? None of you is concerned about me or tells me that my son has incited my servant to lie in wait for me, as he does today."

Thank your two actors and invite them to return to their seats. Then explain that King Saul was jealous of David because he was afraid that David was getting too popular with people and would soon become king. By the way, that is eventually what happened, but it was God's plan, not David's. So Saul was after David, trying to kill him. And here in this passage, read so well by our voice double, King Saul was trying to turn people against David by tearing him down. Eventually, one of the soldiers came forward and confessed where David was. David soon experienced how words can be used to hurt, damage and even destroy people's lives.

Transition to the next step by telling students that as Christians, we should be doing our best to steer clear of damaging conversations.

Option 2: From the Mouths of Babes. For this option, you will need your Bible, copies of "From the Mouths of Babes" (found on the next page) and pens or pencils.

Begin by asking students if they've ever heard this chant: "Sticks and stones may break my bones, but words will never hurt me." Who wrote this? What were they thinking! It should say: "Sticks and stones *might* break my bones, but words will *always* hurt me!" David found this out the hard way.

Read 1 Samuel 22:6-8, and then explain that one of Saul's biggest weapons against David were words. In these verses, we find him trying to turn his men against David. David soon learned that he was in a battle against anger, gossip, lies, jealousy and hate. Saul's words hurt David deeply. In fact, when we read Psalm 12:1-8, we can hear him crying out to God in the midst of the lies and boasts that surround him.

Have everyone say the rhyme with you again: "Sticks and stones may break my bones, but words will never hurt me." Next, distribute "From the Mouths of Babes" and pens or pencils, and have students divide into groups of four or five. Instruct them to rewrite this two-line rhyme, using about the

From the Mouths of Babes

Sticks and stones may break my bones, but words will never hurt me.

Read the following verses from James 3:5-6: "Likewise the tongue is a small part of the body, but it makes great boasts. Consider what a great forest is set on fire by a small spark. The tongue also is a fire, a world of evil among the parts of the body. It corrupts the whole person, sets the whole course of his life on fire, and is itself set on fire by hell."

In light of those verses, work together as a group and write a rhyme to reflect how much words really can hurt!

same amount of words and similar rhythm. Give one or two of the following as examples:

Friends and enemies might make me sad,
* but God will always love me.*

Stabs and jeers might bring me tears,
* but love will always dry them.*

People might laugh behind my back,
* but friends will stand beside me.*

The tongue can hurt when friends are curt,
* but I can rise above them.*

After about five minutes, invite groups to share their rhymes. Praise everyone's efforts and transition to the next step by reading 1 Peter 3:10: "For whoever would love life and see good days must keep his tongue from evil and his lips from deceitful speech." Continue by stating that we will next look at how each of us can do that.

DIG

Option 1: *Home Alone.* You'll need a TV, a DVD player, a copy of the movie *Home Alone*, copies of "Home Alone, Too?" (found on the next page) and pens or pencils.

Ahead of time, cue the video approximately one hour and seven minutes from the beginning to the scene in which Kevin is sitting in the church with the old man who lives on his street. They're having a conversation about family and how unkind words spoken in the past have damaged their relationships. The eight-year-old Kevin offers some great advice to his older neighbor.

Begin the session by viewing the clip, then distribute pens or pencils and "Home Alone, Too?" and invite students to divide into groups of three to complete the statements on the handout. Give them several minutes to work on it and develop their own discussion. Transition to the next step by clarifying that sometimes in relationships, both parties are guilty and someone needs to be the bigger person and make the first move to say I'm sorry. The next step might help us figure out how . . .

Note: For further help in how to say you're sorry, see "How to Say You're Sorry" on pages 97-99.

HOME ALONE, TOO?

In the movie *Home Alone*, Kevin finds out that because of some unkind words spoken many years ago, his neighbor was home alone, too.

What would you do if you were Kevin and his neighbor? The Bible gives great advice. Complete the following statements regarding the old man and his son and Kevin and his mom. Read the Scripture passages and use them to help you respond.

"Therefore, if you are offering your gift at the altar and there remember that your brother has something against you, leave your gift there in front of the altar. First go and be reconciled to your brother; then come and offer your gift" (Matthew 5:23-24).

If I were the old man, I would . . . _____

_____

_____

"Bear with each other and forgive whatever grievances you may have against one another. Forgive as the Lord forgave you" (Colossians 3:13).

If I were his son, I should . . . _____

_____

_____

"Therefore, as God's chosen people, holy and dearly loved, clothe yourselves with compassion, kindness, humility, gentleness and patience" (Colossians 3:12).

If I were Kevin, I really ought to . . . _____

_____

_____

"For if you forgive men when they sin against you, your heavenly Father will also forgive you" (Matthew 6:14).

If I were Kevin's mom, I should . . .

_____

_____

_____

Option 2: Be a Friend. For this option, you need nothing but the story below! Read the following story aloud:

Ken and Courtney have attended the same church since they were both four years old. They're good friends and have a lot of history together. At school, Courtney has a crush on a guy named Scott. He's pretty popular and a ton of girls like him. Ken doesn't know Scott very well, but he does know he has a reputation of "going too far" with a few girls. Ken has even heard him brag about it in the locker room during P.E. class.

One day, Ken is standing at his locker with a few friends when Scott comes up and starts to brag about how he and Courtney got hot and heavy after the game last Friday night. Ken immediately remembers, though, that his mom drove him and Courtney to the youth group pizza party right after the game. Kevin is just about to say something, but all of the guys begin to congratulate Scott, giving him high fives and cheering him on. Ken's mouth freezes and he can't say a thing.

Discuss the following:

- How would you feel if you were Courtney and found out that Ken did not say anything?
- Was Ken just as guilty as Scott?
- What are some things that Ken could say or do to stop the gossip here?
- What would you do if you were Ken?
- How does it make you feel when others defend you?

Explain that it's often hard to know what to say right when you're hearing something like Ken heard about Courtney. That's why you're talking about it ahead of time! If you have time, you may want to role-play some situations to help students prepare for what they face with their friends. Some sample situations might be:

- Brad starts a rumor that Davis stole Billy's skateboard, and Sean, who knows that Davis is innocent, finds out what Brad has been saying.
- Nicole hears Erica telling all the guys that their friend Sharon looked lame in her bathing suit.

Transition to the next step by explaining that in order to *have* a friend, we have to *be* a friend. It might mean that we put an end to gossip by talking kindly about our friends and not joining in on damaging conversations—even if we risk looking bad or being singled out.

APPLY

Option 1: The Encouragement Box. For this option, you need colored notepaper, a shoebox covered with wrapping paper and a slit cut in the top, and pens or pencils.

Distribute colored notepaper to students as you explain that today you've talked about words and their power, and now the students have a chance to use kind words to build someone up.

Give students a few minutes to write a note of encouragement to someone else in your youth ministry. Instruct them to fold up the note, address it to the person they've written it to and place it in the special Encouragement Box (the newly glorified shoebox). You and your team of adult volunteers will deliver the notes after the meeting ends. Be sensitive to students who might not have as many friends and won't be as likely to receive a note from another student by having adult team members write encouragement notes to them.

If students really dive into this activity, you may want to keep the Encouragement Box out for several weeks—some junior-high ministries have kept them out for several years!

Option 2: Talk Show. For this option, you need your Bible, a TV, several 3x5-inch index cards, pens or pencils and transparent tape. Ahead of time, write the following words on separate index cards and tape them to the television screen: "lying," "anger," "rage," "malice," "slander," "filthy language." Then write the following words on different cards and put tape on the back of them: "compassion," "kindness," "humility," "gentleness," "patience," "forgiveness," "love." Be sure to have blank cards for the end of the activity.

Ask, "How many of you would feel comfortable if everything you said was tape-recorded, then played back for everyone to hear? Pretty scary. Well, whether you like it or not, everything that comes out of our mouths is a 'talk' show. So, who stars in your 'talk' show?"

Direct students' attention to the TV and read Colossians 3:8-9. As you read the words you've written on the cards, rip them off the TV. Give the index cards with the tape on the back to several students. Then read Colossians 3:12-14 and invite students with the cards to come up as they hear the word they are holding and tape that card to the TV.

Ask, "In your daily talk show, have you taken off lying, anger, rage, malice, slander and filthy language? Have you put on compassion, kindness, humility, gentleness, patience, forgiveness, love? Who stars in your show?"

Give each student a blank index card. Ask them to write down one way they can avoid gossip this week, using tips from the passage you just looked at. Make tape available so they can tape them to the TV set as a public sign of their commitment to putting on compassion, kindness, humility and all that other good stuff.

Youth Leader Tip

There is probably no social hierarchy that is as strict and well-defined as in the junior-high culture. They become so myopic in their focus on their own identity group that they lose sight of individuality—who each of them is as a unique creation of God.[2]

REFLECT

The following short devotions are for the students to reflect on and answer during the week. You can make a copy of these pages and distribute to your class or print out from the PDF available online at **www.gospellight.com/un common/uncommon_jh_friends_and_peer_pressure.zip**.

1—SAY WHAT?

Read Proverbs 16:28 and see what's stirring.

One day Ginny heard from Sarah that Lara liked Monique's boyfriend, Garrett. She ran up to Monique and asked her if it was true. Monique said she didn't think so, but Ginny went to Garrett and told him that Lara did like him and asked him if he liked her. He told her that Monique was his girlfriend, not Lara. Then Ginny went to Lara and told her that Garrett hated her.

Lara was really hurt so she went to Monique and told her that she really liked Garrett and didn't know why Garrett didn't like her. Monique, thinking that Lara liked her boyfriend as more than a friend, got really angry and told her she didn't think they should be friends anymore. Monique was hurt because she thought Lara was trying to cause trouble and Lara couldn't understand why Monique freaked out like that.

See how gossip can quickly grow out of control? And it only took one person to start the rumors! So don't hang out with gossips, and make sure that you are not a gossip yourself.

Listen to yourself and your friends as you talk today. Are you gossiping? If so, ask God to take control of your mouth and ears. A great standard for gossip is: *If you can't say it to someone's face, don't say it behind his/her back!*

2—GOSSIP, NOT GOSSIP

Read 1 Timothy 6:20 and see where to turn!

Imagine that you're sitting with your friends at the lunch table. What would someone have to say to get you to turn off your ears?

- ❐ These French fries taste like rubber! Do you think they bounce?
- ❐ Did you see the earrings Jaime Tate had on? They were really cute!
- ❐ Andrew is so dumb. He got an *F* on the history quiz!

❏   Dana and I are going to the mall after school. She is so rich.
❏   Hey look! A green potato chip! Gross.

Gossip is interesting and really hard to ignore, but if you value your friend-ships with other people, you will learn to ignore it. What will you do the next time you hear your friends gossiping? Join in? Walk away? Tell them to stop?

3—HANDLE IT LIKE A FRIEND

Look up Proverbs 17:9 and take cover!
Mattie failed her last English test and she was really scared that she would fail the whole class. Her dad thought grades were the most important things in the world and maybe that's why Mattie looked at Jill's paper during their English quiz.
After class, Jill asked to talk with her and she told Mattie that she knew she had cheated. "If you need help, I'll tutor you after school," Jill promised. Mat-tie was really relieved. She told their teacher about the cheating, and although she got an F on that quiz, she got a B on the next one with Jill's help.
Being a friend means helping out no matter what your friend has done to you. It never helps to tell other people how imperfect your buddy is, and that's a pretty quick way to lose that buddy too!

4—ADDICTED TO GOSSIP

Find 2 Timothy 2:16-17 and then look up "gangrene" in the dictionary. Gross!
What piece of gossip would be almost impossible to keep to yourself?

❏   The worst kid in school is about to be expelled.
❏   Your cousin is going to get married secretly.
❏   Your friends are planning on sneaking in to see your favorite band at
     a local coffee house without paying admission.
❏   Your sister took $10 from your brother's wallet.
❏   All the answers to the algebra test this Tuesday are C.

Gossip is totally addicting so don't get involved in it! Stay away from peo-ple that gossip and listen to yourself carefully to make sure you're not talking about other people or your friendships will suffer for it!

JEALOUSY

THE BIG IDEA

Jealousy not only eats away at your friendships—it can eat away at you.

SESSION AIMS

In this session you will guide students to (1) see how jealousy can divide and destroy friendships; (2) learn how to feel good about the successes of their friends; and (3) act by praising one friend for his/her accomplishments.

THE BIGGEST VERSE

"Saul was very angry; this refrain galled him. 'They have credited David with tens of thousands,' he thought, 'but me with only thousands. What more can he get but the kingdom?' And from that time on Saul kept a jealous eye on David" (1 Samuel 18:8).

OTHER IMPORTANT VERSES

Job 1–2; 1 Samuel 16:14; 18:5-16; Proverbs 11:25; Matthew 6:1-2,19-20; 23:5-7; John 13:34-35; Romans 12:15; 1 Corinthians 13:4; Philippians 2:1-4; 1 Thessalonians 5:11

Note: Additional options and worksheets in 8$^1/_2$" x 11" format for this session are available for download at **www.gospellight.com/uncommon/jh_friends_and_peer_pressure.zip**.

STARTER

Option 1: Trash Bag Décor. For this option, you need various popular magazines, scissors, several rolls of transparent tape and several large brown paper bags. Welcome students and introduce this session as another topic on a "friendship wrecker." Divide students into groups of three or four. Distribute a few magazines, transparent tape, a pair of scissors and a paper bag to each group.

Ask them to look through the magazines and cut or rip out anything they see that might be something they want. Clarify that it doesn't have to be a material thing; it could be an ideal like being rich or successful, or maybe they would want someone's cute boyfriend or girlfriend. Encourage them to be creative. Instruct them to tape the images on the paper bag. After several minutes, invite each group to share some of their clippings.

Explain that it's easy to look at what others have and want it for ourselves. This desire can produce feelings of greed, envy and jealousy. When these feelings creep into our friendships, they can eat away at everyone.

There will always be people in our lives who have more or better things than we do. The test of jealousy is not just a question of whether you want it as well but really whether you do *not* want them to have it. *That* is being jealous. Jealousy happens when someone resents an advantage that somebody else has, and although we think of it as something that happens in romantic relationships, it can happen in any relationship. And it has no place in friendships. It should be taken away and thrown out.

Speaking of "throwing out," explain that without knowing it, they have just made "trash" of want and envy. Ask a few students to place these bags around the youth room to use as trash bags until they're ready to be thrown out.

Option 2: Twinkie Day for Girls. For this option, you need enough Twinkies (or other treat) for each student.

Welcome students and introduce this session by explaining that this is another lesson on a "friendship wrecker." Declare that today is "Twinkie Day for

Youth Leader Tip

Most junior-highers feel insecure in their friendships and unsure of who they really are and who they want to be. For students to survive and thrive in junior high, they must *know* that God is with them.[1]

Girls." Every girl present gets a Twinkie because . . . well, just because! Give each girl a Twinkie and invite her to eat and enjoy. The guys will certainly begin to complain and question this terrible unfairness.

Allow for a few moments of this, and then ask the guys: *Why do you think you should get Twinkies, too?* Explain that their responses and feelings are very typical of most people. It's very human of us to want what others have, especially when we feel we deserve it. It's not easy to sit back and watch others prosper, succeed or gain popularity.

Believe it or not, this happens in our friendships, too. Why is it so hard to cheer on our friends and be happy when they're doing well? It may be because we are jealous. Jealousy happens when someone resents an advantage that somebody else has, and although we think of it as something that happens in romantic relationships, it can happen in any relationship, too.

Transition to the next step by explaining that today you're going to check out the way our reaction to the success of others can make or break a friendship. Before you continue, give the guys Twinkies too.

MESSAGE

Option 1: *The Princess Bride.* For this option, you will need several Bibles, a television set, a DVD player, a copy of the classic movie *The Princess Bride* and candy for prizes.

Ahead of time, cue the video approximately one hour and four minutes from the beginning to the scene where Princess Buttercup and Prince Humperdink are having a conversation in Prince Humperdink's chambers about sending out the four fastest ships in his armada. Princess Buttercup then goes into a short monologue about the true love between her and Westley. Humperdink is so filled with jealousy and rage that he goes to the "Pit of Despair" to kill Westley. Also read 1 Samuel 18:5-16 several times so you're familiar with all of the details.

Introduce the clip by explaining that Prince Humperdink is jealous of the true love between Westley and Buttercup—so much so that he can't stand the possibility of them ever being together. Begin the clip and stop it after Westley's long moan.

After viewing the clip, explain that, as you just witnessed in this clip, jealousy can drive people to dangerous actions. In the case of Prince Humperdink, he was so jealous of the relationship between Westley and Princess Buttercup that he wanted Westley dead.

Explain that the Bible tells a story about a jealous king. His name was Saul. Saul and David were friends. Saul wanted David around and even gave him promotions. But then something happened—everyone started liking David better than they liked King Saul.

David was a handsome, skilled musician and a great warrior; in fact, he had just killed the Philistine giant, Goliath. Not only that, but the Bible says over and over again that "God was with him." People grew to love, respect and admire David and Saul didn't like it one bit. He wanted the attention and favor of the public, but David kept getting it. King Saul grew jealous—jealous enough to want David dead.[2] Talk about a friendship wrecker!

Distribute Bibles and ask volunteers to read one or two verses from 1 Samuel 18:5-16 aloud until the passage is read in full. Explain that you've studied this story ahead of time, and now you're going to play "Stump the Teacher." Students can ask you any question that can be answered by the passage, and if you can't answer it, you'll give them some candy.

Do this for several minutes, then transition to the next step by emphasizing that jealousy can destroy and divide friends. One way to combat jealousy is to feel good when our friends succeed instead of wanting them to fail. Let's look at how we can do that . . .

Option 2: Yearbook Glory. For this option, you need several Bibles and one or two school yearbooks from your students.

Ahead of time, ask to borrow a couple of your students' yearbooks (or use one of yours, if you dare!). Before students arrive, go through the yearbooks and note any pictures of groups or individuals that appear several times throughout the book. If you have more than 10 students, consider making a PowerPoint or Keynote slideshow of several pages ahead of time.

As students arrive, instruct them to sit cross-legged on the floor in a semicircle. In "storybook reading" fashion, show the yearbook, pointing out notable photos. If the person who owns the book is there, ask him or her to comment on the photos and the people in them. Ask, "How do you feel when you get your yearbook, look through it and don't find many—or any—pictures of yourself, yet there are lots of pictures of some of your friends?"

Share your own experiences of opening your yearbook for the first time, wondering if you "made it in." Explain that sometimes when our friends succeed and others pay attention to them, we might feel jealous. Yearbooks can be a reminder of who the school pays more attention to—and when it's not us, it hurts.

Explain that there's a story in the Bible about two friends whose relationship was ruined because of a similar experience; one got a lot more attention than the other. At the start, Saul, who was king, liked David a lot. He wanted him around all the time and even promoted him.

Saul called on David to play the harp for him when he was feeling down. Not only was David a great musician, but he was also a skilled warrior, a quick learner, good looking and God was blessing him. Eventually, the people grew to love, respect and admire David, especially after he killed the Philistine giant, Goliath. That would have assured him a huge picture in any newspaper, tabloid or yearbook!

But Saul was king! He wanted the attention and favor of the public, and yet David kept getting it. Everyone loved David, not just for killing the enemy giant Goliath, but for being a great guy. King Saul became jealous.

Invite students to turn in their Bibles to 1 Samuel 18:5-16 and assign several to read part of the passage. Then ask the group why Saul went from liking David to being jealous of him. (*He felt threatened that others would like David more; he wanted all of the attention; David got credit that Saul wanted; he wanted to be the only one who succeeded.*)

Transition to the next step by emphasizing that jealousy can destroy and divide friends. One way to combat jealousy is to feel good when our friends succeed instead of wanting them to fail. Let's look at how we can do that . . .

DIG

Option 1: Complimentary Compliments. For this option, you need copies of "Complimentary Compliments" (found on the next page) and pens and pencils. Introduce this next step by explaining that because jealousy is a sure way to wreck a friendship, we should do what we can to avoid it or get rid of it. Learning to appreciate our friends and praise their accomplishments is a great repair kit.

Youth Leader Tip

For most students, junior high is a time of notorious cruelty, resulting in paralyzing fear of being different. The in-crowd excludes. Nicknames abound. Popularity controls. Help your students to live up to Jesus' example of kindness.[3]

Complimentary Compliments

Learning to give praise and appreciation takes practice. This activity will help you practice the art of complimenting others when they succeed.

Your best friend gets asked to the dance by the cutest girl/guy in your class. You were hoping it would happen to you.

You cheer him/her on by saying . . .

_____

You and your friend stay up late studying for the big science test. Your friend gets an A- and you get a C+.

You praise your friend by . . .

_____

Your friend is running for class president. He/she is getting a lot of attention lately and you feel a little left out. You hear some classmates talking about how great your friend would be as class president.

You support your friend by saying . . .

_____

You and your friend audition for the big school musical. Your friend gets the lead part and you get a small supporting role.

You encourage and applaud your friend by . . .

_____

Ask for a volunteer to read Philippians 2:1-4. Distribute pens or pencils and "Complimentary Compliments" and give students five minutes to complete the handout. Next, have students divide into groups of three or four and discuss their answers. Transition to the next step by explaining that now they will have an opportunity to try this out for real!

Option 2: In the Limelight. For this option, you need a Bible and the story below. Read the following story:

Reid and Luke are great friends and both serve on the student council. Reid was nominated to be in charge of coordinating the eighth-grade dance and Luke offered to help him in any way he could. Luke and Reid met a few times to discuss the details and divide up the responsibilities evenly. Between them, they came up with the theme, coordinated all the decorations, lined up chaperones, scheduled the DJ and made all the arrangements for the refreshments.

The dance turned out to be a blast! Everything ran smoothly and it was the most successful dance of the year. Everyone was commenting on how much fun they were having and no one wanted to go home. Before the end of the evening, the vice principal called Reid up to the stage to publicly thank him and congratulate him on a great job. The whole school cheered him on. Afterward, Reid went to Luke and thanked him for his help.

Discuss the following question: *How would you feel if you were Luke?* After a short discussion, read from Romans 12:15: "Rejoice with those who rejoice; mourn with those who mourn." Reid was the coordinator of the dance and it was his job to make it happen whether he did it himself or asked for the help of others. In light of this, how should Luke respond to the attention and applause Reid received for the success of the dance?

Ask students to put themselves in Luke's shoes and give examples of praise and compliments that he could give to Reid, as well as encouragement that Reid could give to Luke.

APPLY

Option 1: A Walk Through the Forest. For this option, you need copies of "A Walk Through the Forest" (found on the following page) and pens or pencils.

A Walk Through the Forest

Praise and encouragement can be like glue that keeps friends together. Try to identify someone in your group who resembles one of the following statements:

_____
is like a *path*—always pointing us in the right direction and showing us the way to go.

_____
is like a *tree*—standing tall, strong and firm no matter what happens.

_____
is like a *cool stream*—helping us feel better when things get dry and boring.

_____
is like a *tent*—making us feel at home.

_____
is like a *wildflower*—adding color and joy to our group.

_____
is like *sunshine*—lots of energy and always warm and giving.

_____
is like an *open meadow*—a calm and quiet spirit that helps us relax.

Distribute pens or pencils and "A Walk Through the Forest" and give students a few minutes to complete it. Then allow them to share their responses and give each other encouragement, praise and honor.

Close by praying for the friendships in the youth group and ask God to help students to be givers of joy and approval rather than jealousy and envy.

Option 2: Certificate of Appreciation. For this option, you need copies of "Certificate of Appreciation" (found on the folowing page) and pens or pencils.

Distribute pens or pencils and "Certificate of Appreciation" to students. Explain that they have an opportunity to counteract any feelings of jealousy by giving praise and appreciation to one friend. Give them several minutes to complete the handout and encourage them to give it to a friend this week.

Close the lesson by praying for forgiveness for any feelings of jealousy and envy in our friendships.

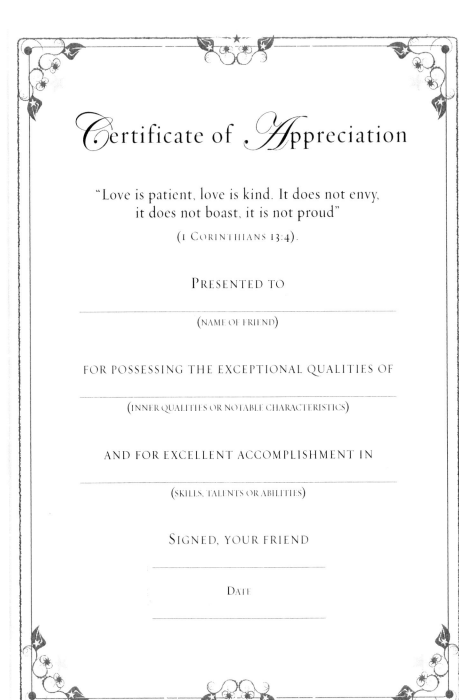

Certificate of Appreciation

"Love is patient, love is kind. It does not envy,
it does not boast, it is not proud"

(1 Corinthians 13:4).

PRESENTED TO

_____

(NAME OF FRIEND)

FOR POSSESSING THE EXCEPTIONAL QUALITIES OF

_____

(INNER QUALITIES OR NOTABLE CHARACTERISTICS)

AND FOR EXCELLENT ACCOMPLISHMENT IN

_____

(SKILLS, TALENTS OR ABILITIES)

SIGNED, YOUR FRIEND

_____

DATE

_____

REFLECT

The following short devotions are for the students to reflect on and answer during the week. You can make a copy of these pages and distribute to your class or print out from the PDF available online at **www.gospellight.com/un common/uncommon_jh_friends_and_peer_pressure.zip**.

1—LIKE YOURSELF, LIKE YOUR FRIENDS

Find James 3:13-18 and don't brag about it!

Will wished he could play baseball like Steven or be really good at science like Gina or play piano like Hope. Will whined and complained, constantly telling his friends that he wished he were like them—until they were all sick of hearing it. Instead of learning to do something like play the flute or dance the latest dance, he began to really dislike his friends. *It's not fair!* he thought. *They're all a bunch of showoffs. What jerks!*

Admiring your friends and enjoying the talents God gave them is fun, but being jealous is another thing entirely. It's easy to become jealous when you don't totally like who you are or what you can do.

Pray for God to give you peace and appreciation about who you are and to help you enjoy and encourage the friends He has given you!

2—BE GOOD, NOT BETTER

Read Proverbs 14:30 to find out if there's something rotten in here.

What is one thing you would love to be able to do?

- ❒ Play baseball better than Babe Ruth
- ❒ Dance like one of the famous ballet dancers
- ❒ Stop time by touching your index finger to your nose
- ❒ Be a famous actor and win an Oscar
- ❒ Sing better than any famous rock star

Wanting to do something well is cool, but when you focus all your energy on being better than someone else, that person becomes your enemy. It's really hard to love someone you're always trying to outdo!

Do yourself a favor—don't try to be better than any of your friends. Thank God for putting them in your life and be the best *you* that you can be!

3—DON'T COMPARE!

Don't delay, but check out 1 Corinthians 13:4.

Megan and Juanita have been friends since they were five years old and met at Sunday School. Now that they're in junior high, they've both changed a lot. For instance, Juanita has a beautiful singing voice and does solos at school and in front of the entire church sometimes. Juanita also really likes to be a leader, so she joined the ministry team and now she helps plan bake sales and overnighters and car washes. Everybody thinks she's a really great Christian and Megan is beginning to feel left out and envious of Juanita. *After all*, Megan thinks, *she's not that perfect.*

Comparing yourself to your friends is never a good idea! You'll end up disliking yourself and losing your friends or being full of pride, thinking you're better than your friends.

God made all of us special with different talents and abilities so that we can work together. What are two special talents that you have that you can use this week?

_____

_____

_____

_____

_____

_____

_____

4—ENVY IS A DEAD END

Go to Romans 16:17-19 and get ready to party!

Imagine you're at a party. The first person you meet is reading magazines, and as she looks through them, she comments on how this model has the perfect nose, that one has perfect hair and that model has a perfect body. How would you begin to feel about the way you look?

The next person you meet is a guy who is talking about a pair of $300 basketball shoes that he's going to get with lights and space-age materials and glow-in-the-dark soles. How would you begin to think about your shoes?

The next person you meet is watching MTV, talking about how if you don't dress like the people on MTV, you just ain't cool. How would you begin to feel about your clothes?

Do you think hanging out with envious people is a good idea or a bad one? Why do you think this way?

_____

_____

_____

_____

_____

_____

_____

_____

Are you happy with who you are? Why or why not?

_____

_____

_____

_____

_____

_____

_____

Are your friends happy with who you are? How do you know?

_____

_____

_____

_____

_____

_____

_____

_____

If you hang out with people who are always complaining about how they don't have cool clothes or the right house, their attitudes will start to rub off on you and make you unhappy with your life and yourself. Ask God to help you and your friends to be content with everything He has given you.

UNRESOLVED ANGER

THE BIG IDEA

Unresolved anger can put an end to even the best of friendships.

SESSION AIMS

In this session you will guide students to (1) learn that anger is powerful and can bring an end to friendships; (2) feel the desire to resolve anger in their friendships; and (3) act by forgiving their friends who make them angry.

THE BIGGEST VERSE

"For Saul said to himself, 'I will not raise a hand against him. Let the Philistines do that!'" (1 Samuel 18:17).

OTHER IMPORTANT VERSES

1 Samuel 18:10-17,20-29; 19–20:42; Proverbs 12:16; 15:1; 29:11; Matthew 5:23-24,44; Ephesians 4:26-27,31; Colossians 3:13; James 1:19

Note: Additional options and worksheets in 8¹/₂" x 11" format for this session are available for download at **www.gospellight.com/uncommon/jh_friends_and_peer_pressure.zip**.

STARTER

Option 1: Anger Demo. For this option, you will need one adult staff member or volunteer. Ahead of time, get together with the volunteer and go through the following anger scenario. As students are gathering together, begin the confrontation:

> **You**: Hey, _____ did you pick up the chocolate bars I asked you to get?
>
> **Volunteer** (nonchalantly): No, sorry, I didn't get around to it.
>
> **You** (quite miffed): You could have let me know! I would have done it myself if I knew you couldn't do it.
>
> **Volunteer**: I didn't think it was that big a deal . . .
>
> **You** (quickly snapping): I *told* you I needed it for our youth meeting today. I *said* it was part of the lesson! Now I can't do what I had planned!
>
> **Volunteer**: Sorry! I didn't think you'd get so upset!
>
> **You**: Of course I'm upset! I called you ahead of time and made these plans and now they've fallen through. You've ruined everything!

At this point, the two of you can stop and let the group in on the scheme. Explain that today you're going to talk about anger and how it can affect friendships. Say to the group, "[Name of volunteer] and I just gave you a taste of how anger can creep into everyday life. It's a powerful emotion, and if we're not careful, it can ruin even the best of friendships." Read Ephesians 4:26-27. Tell that grup that we learn from this passage that anger itself is not a sin, but it can become a sin if we don't handle it well. So let's learn together how to handle it well . . .

Option 2: Rate Your Rage. For this option, you need copies of "Rate Your Rage" (found on the next page) and pens or pencils.

Greet students and introduce this lesson by explaining that you'll be talking today about anger and how it affects friendships. First, you're all going to rate your own anger levels. Distribute pens or pencils and "Rate Your Rage" and allow students a couple of minutes to complete the handout. Discuss each situation and encourage students to share why they gave themselves the ratings that they did. Invite them to share their total Rage Rate with the rest of the group.

Use the following statements to rate how mad you might get in certain situations.

RATE YOUR RAGE

You're grounded all weekend for not taking out the garbage and you had big plans.

Upset **Very Bothered** **Angry**

1 2 3 4 5 6 7 8 9 10

Your friends go to a movie together and didn't bother to call you.

Upset **Very Bothered** **Angry**

1 2 3 4 5 6 7 8 9 10

A seam ripped while you were wearing the new pair of jeans you just bought.

Upset **Very Bothered** **Angry**

1 2 3 4 5 6 7 8 9 10

You're walking down the hall at school and someone purposely trips you.

Upset **Very Bothered** **Angry**

1 2 3 4 5 6 7 8 9 10

Add your numbered rankings and list your score:

_____ is your Rage Rate.

Transition to the next step by explaining that anger is a powerful emotion. It affects how we feel and act toward others. The good news is that the Bible has a lot to say about anger. Read Ephesians 4:26-27. We learn in this passage that anger itself is not a sin, but it can become a sin if we don't handle it well. So let's learn together how to handle it well . . .

MESSAGE

Option 1: Vehicles of Anger. For this option, you will need your Bible, copies of "Vehicles of Anger" (found on the following page) and pens or pencils for everyone in the group.

Begin by explaining that just as a car accident can be anything from a scratch to a full-fledged collision, we tend to express our anger in anything from a cutting remark to acts of physical violence. Ask students to get into groups of three or four and distribute pens or pencils and "Vehicles of Anger." Instruct them to spend a couple of minutes reading it over, circling which kind of car accident they would be, and then sharing what they circled with the rest of their group.

Call the students back together and explain that in the continuing story about David and King Saul, we find that Saul's feelings of jealousy have turned into fits of rage and violence.

Next, read 1 Samuel 18:10-16. Ask, "In this passage, how would you describe Saul's anger in relation to a 'vehicle of anger'? In 1 Samuel 18:29, we learn that 'Saul became still more afraid of him, and he remained his enemy the rest of his days.' Saul and David used to be friends. How did Saul's anger affect their friendship?" (*It caused fear and resentment and kept them apart because David had to flee to protect his life.*)

Transition to the next step by explaining that anger is a human emotion and most of us experience anger at some point in our friendships. That's bad news. The good news is that there are ways to resolve it!

Youth Leader Tip

Right and wrong are two words that are becoming more and more foreign to today's teens. What is right is what God asks us to do. What is wrong is doing the opposite. The key is to help your students choose to *act* on what they know is right.[1]

JUST A SCRATCH:

You barely notice! It can be rubbed out in no time. (You're not quick to notice when others do wrong.)

FENDER BENDER:

A sure hit, but not too strong; a little repair will make it like new. (When you get angry, you resolve it and make things better.)

SIDESWIPED:

The other person doesn't even see your anger coming and—BAM!—you lash out, a total surprise! (You hold it in for too long and don't deal with it right away, and then you overreact to the slightest thing.)

VEHICLES OF ANGER

How do you deal with anger? Well, let's say you are a car. If you get angry, your anger shows in one of the following ways:

REAR-END COLLISION:

You impact others from behind. (You tell others instead of the person you are mad at. You're afraid to confront someone who has hurt you.)

HEAD-ON COLLISION:

You cause a heavy full-on impact with lots of damage. (You tend to blow up and speak without thinking, causing terrible damage to the friendship.)

Option 2: Icy Rage. For this option, you need your Bible and a bag of ice cubes in a small cooler.

1. *Anger can hurt.* Give each student a piece of ice and ask him or her to hold on to it while you read 1 Samuel 18:10-17,29. Then explain that Saul's anger toward David went beyond feelings. It moved into actions—in fact, violent actions. Saul was so afraid, jealous and angry at David that he tried to kill him—not just once, but many times!

   Invite students to try to hold on tightly to the piece of ice in their hand. See how long they can keep their fists closed before it hurts and they let go.

   Explain that, eventually, the coldness of the ice hurts. That's exactly what happened to Saul's anger towards David. Saul didn't let go of the anger and it finally became painful. The same can happen in our friendships. But there is a way to resolve it.

2. *Anger can destroy.* Ask students to continue to hold their ice cubes as you explain that hail is a little thing that can devastate crops, injure animals, pound people, damage aircraft and dent cars. These ice balls come in all sizes, from a tiny pellet to the size of a grapefruit. Hail is formed when a cloud is blown by a violent wind, causing it to rise into the freezing zone in the atmosphere. At that point, ice builds up around the nucleus of a snow pellet. The higher and longer the thunderstorm tosses the particles around, the larger and more destructive the hailstones become, until eventually they are so heavy that they fall to the ground.

   The piece of ice that the students are holding in their hands could easily be the size of actual hail. Although it would have started as a tiny pellet of moisture, it would grow in size as it got bounced around.

   Hail from a thundercloud and a person's anger have a lot in common. If feelings of anger are not resolved, violent winds of bitterness and hurt feelings can carry the level of anger higher and higher and make it grow even bigger. Pretty soon the feelings of anger get so heavy that they spill out in verbal or even physical attacks on others, either directly or behind their backs. If these feelings of anger are not dealt with, they grow into actions of anger that can damage a friendship, just like a hailstorm can damage property and people.

3. *Forgiveness can heal.* Ask: *What's happening to the ice cube in your hand the longer you hold it?* (It's melting.) Exactly! There are things we can do to melt our anger toward a friend. One of the best things to do is to *forgive.* Friendships are restored when friends forgive each other for the pain caused when they were angry at each other.

DIG

Option 1: Hot Potato. For this option, you need several boiled or baked potatoes, one for every three to four students. Plan accordingly, because the potatoes need to be hot by the time you reach this step. You can wrap them in towels and brown paper bags to keep them warm for 20 to 30 minutes. Yes, it's more work, but it makes a good point!

Divide students into groups of four or five and tell them they are going to share about the last time they got mad, which may very well have been earlier that day. It can be anything from "My brother made us late for school this morning because he dumped his cereal bowl" to "My math teacher gave us a ton of homework and it's due tomorrow."

Here's the catch. Each group is going to be handed a very hot potato. The first person who gets it begins sharing but can only talk as long as they are holding the potato. As soon as they pass it to the next person, it becomes his or her turn to share, and so on. The hot potato continues to get passed around the group, and since they can only talk when they're holding the potato, it may take several rounds to finish a story.

During the first round, students will only be able to blurt out one or two words before they have to toss it to the next person. Eventually the potato will cool down and they'll be able to hold it longer and finish their story.

Allow enough time after the potatoes have cooled for the groups to discuss anger, and then explain that anger is like a hot potato—it's hard to deal with when it's so hot! Once our anger cools down, it's easier to deal with in a gentle and logical manner. Sometimes it's best to let our anger cool before dealing with the issue. Proverbs 29:11 warns us that "a fool gives full vent to his anger, but a wise man keeps himself under control," and in Proverbs 12:16 we learn that "a fool shows his annoyance at once, but a prudent man overlooks an insult." How does this relate to the hot potato? Once we cool down, we'll be better able to deal with our anger in the right way.

Option 2: Reactions to Anger. For this option, you need copies of "Reactions to Anger" (found on the following two pages) and pens or pencils.

Ask students to listen carefully as you read the story on the handout. Explain as you distribute pens or pencils and "Reactions to Anger" that each of these friends reacted to Scott in a different way. Invite students to try to identify who's who. (The answers are: "the Clam" is Kalyn; "the Outburst" is Jamie; "the Avenger" is Brandon; "the Accuser" is Curtis; and "the Diplomat" is Meagan.)

After a few minutes, ask students to share their answers. As volunteers share their responses, have each one choose another student to read the Scripture verse that follows his/her answer.

Transition to the next step by asking students to silently choose a description that best fits them. Then explain that anger is a part of our human makeup. Though it may not be a sin to become angry, our reactions often become sinful, as Paul reminds us in Ephesians 4:26,27: "In your anger do not sin . . . do not give the devil a foothold."

APPLY

Option 1: A Cure for Anger. For this option, you need one adhesive bandage for each student.

Begin by explaining that anger can easily creep into any relationship. It's a part of life because it's a part of our human nature, but it does not excuse us to express words that hurt. Instead, we should find ways to cure our anger and mend the relationship.

Distribute the adhesive bandages to students as you challenge them to stick this bandage in a pocket or somewhere where they'll have immediate

Youth Leader Tip

Even after we are saved by Christ, we are still tempted to sin. Yet in the midst of our sin and our humanity, God uses us. Remind your students that they can use their abilities to praise God and serve others in the midst of their sin, weakness and timidity.[2]

Reactions to Anger?

Jamie, Kalyn, Curtis, Meagan and Brandon were all good friends. They had grown up together and were now in the seventh grade. Jamie's older brother Scott promised to drive all of them to the mountains the upcoming weekend to ski. They had been planning this trip for over a month and couldn't wait to go.

Two days before the trip, Jamie called all of her friends to tell them that Scott had changed his mind and was spending the weekend with friends from out of town. Jamie's first response to her brother was outrage and harsh words. She yelled at him and blamed him for ruining the whole weekend for her and her friends.

After school the next day, all of her friends came over to her house. Scott was sitting on the living-room couch when they came in. When he said hi to Kalyn, she looked right at him, didn't answer and turned away. Curtis, however, confronted him and said, "That's pretty rude of you to let us down like that. You ruined our whole weekend. Thanks a lot!" Meagan, on the other hand, tried to talk to Scott and ask him why he changed his mind. She really wanted answers.

As they were all leaving that night, Brandon took out his house key and made a small scratch on Scott's car on his way out. No one saw him do it.

Read the descriptions below and match them up with the characters in the story: Jamie, Meagan, Brandon, Kalyn and Curtis.

The Clam: This is the type of person who "clams up" when they're mad. They give the "cold-shoulder treatment" and non-verbal signs that they're upset. When it comes to being angry, they tend to hold it in instead of dealing with it.

Ephesians 4:31: "Get rid of all bitterness, rage and anger, brawling and slander, along with every form of malice."

The Outburst: This person doesn't usually think before they speak. Displays of rage and anger are usually their first response to conflict. Their outbursts can be anything from hurtful words to throwing a shoe.

James 1:19: "My dear brothers, take note of this: Everyone should be quick to listen, slow to speak and slow to become angry."

The Accuser: This person is one who wants to confront, usually with the intent of accusing. They are "in your face" when it comes to being angry. They don't ignore the situation, but can usually keep their cool. However, they're quick to point the finger.

Colossians 3:13: "Bear with each other and forgive whatever grievances you may have against one another. Forgive as the Lord forgave you."

The Avenger: This person can be dangerous when anger sets in. They tend to express their anger by acts of destruction and sometimes violence. Unlike "the Outburst," their actions are thought out with revenge and retaliation in mind. Most times they later regret their actions, but by then it's too late; the damage has been done.

Ephesians 4:26-27: "In your anger do not sin. Do not let the sun go down while you are still angry, and do not give the devil a foothold."

The Diplomat: This person likes to get to the bottom of the problem by talking. They are confrontational in a diplomatic sort of way and want to make sure they have all the facts before coming to a judgment.

Proverbs 15:1: "A gentle answer turns away wrath, but a harsh word stirs up anger."

access to it during the next week. The next time they get angry with a friend, before they speak or respond in any way, they should take out the bandage, open it and place it on the back of their right hand where they'll see it the rest of the day.

This will remind students to keep quiet until they calm down so that they don't immediately react in their anger. Not only that, it will be a visual reminder later in the day to go back and deal with the situation. By that time, hopefully their anger will have cooled down, and then they'll be able to resolve the situation without such strong feelings of anger.

Close the lesson by praying that God would give students the strength to control their reactions to anger and avoid any damage to their friendships.

Option 2: Change for a Dime. For this option, you will need one dime for each student in the group.

Distribute one dime to each student. Now that you've discussed anger, how it can hurt and how to deal with it, explain that you're going to give everyone a challenge. Invite them to hold the dime and look at it as you give these instructions:

> You've heard the phrase, "Count to 10." Well, here's a way to count to 10, but it will take much longer. The next time you become angry with someone, take out the dime and ask around for change for a dime. You're not allowed to talk to the person who made you angry until you find change for the dime, and here's the clincher: It must be 10 pennies—no nickels allowed.
>
> When you finally get 10 pennies, return to your friend and ask her to hold out her hand. Give her a penny, and as you do, state one reason why you like her and what makes her such a good friend. Do this until you have used up all 10 pennies, giving her 10 reasons. At the end, confess to her that you were angry and why you were angry and tell her you forgive her. It's possible that your friend might end up getting mad at you if you act as if you are better than her, so make sure you continue to affirm her and your friendship the whole time.

This is a challenging exercise, but tell students that you have confidence that they have the maturity to count to 10!

Close the session by praying for strong, mature friendships and that God would help us to forgive so that we can be forgiven.

REFLECT

The following short devotions are for the students to reflect on and answer during the week. You can make a copy of these pages and distribute to your class or print out from the PDF available online at **www.gospellight.com/un common/uncommon_jh_friends_and_peer_pressure.zip.**

1—FIGHTIN' WORDS

Hey! Don't blink until you've read Matthew 5:21-22!

In Eli's family, there's a fight almost every day. Everyone yells and curses and tells each other to shut up. So when Eli fights with his friends, he fights the same way, yelling and screaming and calling them foul names. "It's no big deal," he tells his friend Pat when Pat tells him that's a bad way to argue. "That's how I've fought all my life, and besides, it's not like I mean it when I call you names. Don't be so sensitive."

Lots of people do things they regret later when they're upset with someone, especially when that someone is a friend or family member. When you fight with your friends (and everybody eventually does) are you as calm and honest as you can be?

_____

_____

_____

_____

_____

_____

_____

Do you try to hurt your friend the way he or she hurt you, calling him or her names and being cruel?

_____

_____

_____

_____

_____

_____

_____

Ask God to help you love your friends, even when they do something that hurts you.

2—STICKS AND STONES

Race to James 1:19-21 and see what God desires for you!

What would you feel and do if your best friend said something like this to you?

- "I don't even know why I'm friends with you. You're so dumb sometimes!"
- "Can't you see I'm trying to read? Quit bugging me already!"
- "You don't know anything about it, so why don't you just shut up?"

Ouch! Some of those things would be really hard to take! If this person really is your friend, however, you need to remember that we're all imperfect. They may be angry at someone else but are taking it out on you. Walk away when they're like that or just ignore them.

Think of what you do when you're angry. Do you fly off the handle and say hurtful things?

_____

_____

_____

_____

_____

_____

Do you need to apologize to anyone today for the things you've said when you were mad?

_____

_____

_____

_____

_____

3—DON'T LET THE SUN GO DOWN

Get into Ephesians 4:25-27 and see what to do before sunset every day!

Pam slammed the phone down before Erin could say any more. She was so ticked! How could Erin have been such a jerk—telling Lance that Pam liked him! The next day at school Pam refused to talk to her, and when Erin tried to apologize, Pam turned around and walked away. Pam wouldn't pick up the phone when she called all that weekend and pretty soon Erin stopped trying to call. At school, they wouldn't even look at each other. A few months later, it was summer and Pam missed Erin and Erin missed Pam, but it was too late. It seemed their relationship might be too damaged to repair.

Don't let that happen to you! Listen to your friends when they want to apologize, even if you still feel hurt. Accept their apologies and take the opportunity to talk things out. And when you hurt one of your friends, do everything you can to make it right.

4—ALL THE TIME

Dive into Proverbs 17:17 and see what a friend is.

When is it easiest to love your friends?

❑ When they bring you a plate of warm chocolate-chip cookies?
❑ When they help you clean your room?
❑ When they tell you they love being your friend?

When is it hardest to love your friends?

❑ When they ignore you?
❑ When they give one of your secrets away?
❑ When you get in a big fight?

When do your friends need your love the most?

❑ When their parents are fighting?
❑ When they're feeling alone?
❑ When they think no one else loves them?

Loving someone all the time is a pretty tall order, especially if your friends have hurt you or pushed you away. God is the only one who can give us what we need to give love like that. Ask God to help you show your friends that you care about them today.

HOW TO SAY YOU'RE SORRY

Words by themselves are cheap! The only way to truly say you're sorry is to change the actions that offended God or another person. That's what the Bible refers to as repentance (see Acts 26:20).

It's only through the process of repentance that we can seek forgiveness, and it's only through God's forgiveness that we are cleansed of our sins. The following letter was written to a man on death row by the father of the man he killed. When you're done reading the letter, try to figure out which famous father might have written it.

You are probably surprised that I, of all people, am writing a letter to you. But as the father of the man you helped to murder, I have something very important to say to you: I forgive you.

With all my heart, I forgive you. I realize it may be hard for you to believe, but I really do. At your trial, when you showed your sorrow for your part in the events that cost my son his life and asked for my forgiveness, I immediately granted you that forgiving love. I can only hope you believe me and will accept my forgiveness.

But that is not all I have to say to you. I want to make you an offer. I want you to become my adopted child. You see, my son who died was my only child, and now I want to share my life with you and leave my riches to you.

This may not make sense to you or anyone else, but I believe you are worth the offer. I have arranged matters so that if you will receive my offer of forgiveness, not only will you be pardoned for your crime, but your death sentence will be dismissed and you will be set free from your imprisonment. You will become my adopted child and heir to all my riches.

Have you guessed who this famous father is? Turn the page upside down to read the answer.

Maybe you guessed who the father was or maybe you didn't, but the truth is that once you repent to God for whatever you've done, He wipes the sin away—it's gone. And so is that guilty feeling you have when you know you've done something wrong (see 1 John 1:9). That's why you should admit your misdeeds to God—or to anyone else, for that matter.

But what about figuring out how to say you're sorry?

THREE BIG STEPS

The word Jesus uses for saying you're sorry is "repent," which means to "turn from sin." When you do something wrong, you take these three big steps in repenting:

1. You admit your mistake, taking ownership over it.
2. You turn from it and change your actions, so that you don't repeat it.
3. You seek restitution to correct the wrongdoing.

For example, let's say you borrowed your best friend's sweatshirt and carelessly spilled grape juice all over it and can't get the stain out. First, tell your friend about your mistake, apologizing for your carelessness (taking ownership). Second, promise to be more careful in the future (changing your actions), and third, ask your friend how you can replace his/her sweatshirt—buy him/her a new one or maybe give him/her one of your favorites (restitution). Get it?

THE FATHER IS GOD

TWO BIG TYPES

There are two big types of things that you might need to be sorry for. Here are some examples and appropriate actions to take to repent.

When you've done something wrong.

1. You gossiped about a new kid in school. Remove yourself from all gossip and introduce yourself to the kid, remembering that you are an example of Jesus' love.

2. You were swearing during a football game at P.E. Ask God for forgiveness and make sure to use your words to honor Him in the future!

When you haven't done something right.

1. A new student at your school dropped his tray during lunch to-day. You didn't laugh at him like everyone else, but you also didn't help him out because the other students might laugh at you, too. The next time you see someone who needs a helping hand, be the first in line to help!

2. You didn't pray before you headed off to school. Tomorrow, set your alarm five minutes earlier and plan to spend that extra time with God.

ONE BIG ACTION

Every day you will do something wrong or you won't do something right, which can hurt your friends and take you further away from God. The more you use the steps of repentance, the more repentance becomes a habit. The more repentance becomes a habit, the easier it is.

Throughout history, God has done big things like resolving arguments, ending addictions and mending broken hearts—all because someone recognized their own wrongdoing and repented. Anyone—even you—who learns to say "I'm sorry" to God, family and friends can be part of a new revival in a family, church, school or city.

What an awesome opportunity you have!

UNIT II

Peer Pressure

Imagine standing shoulder to shoulder with eight others in front of a classroom of peers. You've been told you're there for a psychological experiment in visual judgment. You are shown two white cards: One contains a single dark, vertical line; the other has three vertical lines of various lengths. Your job? Choose the line on the second card that is the same length as the line on the first card. You think to yourself, *No sweat, this is easy. It's line* C. However, the six people who answer ahead of you choose line *B*. Now the pressure is on. Do you go along with the majority and choose line *B*, even when you are pretty confident it's line *C*, or do you stand up for your own minority opinion?

If you're like the college students who were originally involved in this well-known experiment conducted by S. E. Asch, you'll go along with the crowd one-third of the time. What you don't realize is that the previous six who have answered before you have all been instructed ahead of time to lie and choose an incorrect answer. What you *do* realize is that if you answer based on your own convictions, you'll be the only one saying line *C*, and you wouldn't want to be in that position, would you?

Now rewind in your memory to what you were like as a junior-higher. You're not always as sure about what the right thing is, and even if you are, you certainly don't want to be the only one doing it.

We've carefully designed this unit around three basic principles to help your junior-highers know what the right thing to do is, and then stand up and do it.

1. *The power of one.* Here's a true/false statement: It takes a rare junior-higher to stand up to the pressures to cheat, swear, become physically intimate, experiment with drugs and alcohol, or talk back to his or her parents. On the surface, the statement is true, but maybe a truer statement would be: It takes a junior-higher connected to a rare God to stand up to the pressures that bear down upon them. Your students will find it extremely difficult to muster their own strength to say no when everyone around them

is saying yes. Apart from God, that is. (And even with God, it's not always easy!)

Perhaps you've heard the expression, "God plus one equals a majority." Actually, that's quite heretical. With or without anybody else, God is a majority. Period. In this book, we have tried to give your students all sorts of ideas to build their relationship with God so that they can become more aware of what it means to be on God's side.

2. *The power of a few.* Too many junior-highers feel alone in their struggles with peer pressure. Sure, they hear that junior-highers in general struggle with doing the right thing, but that's too abstract. They need time to hear about Suzie's struggles with cheating, Max's difficulties in knowing how to respond to the crude jokes he hears in P.E. and Jordan's confusion about how much he should be kissing his new girlfriend, especially since she seems to want to do it a lot. Please, please, please take advantage of the small-group options in these lessons so that students can wrestle together with what it means to obey God in an ungodly world, until they eventually—hopefully—pin it down.

3. *The power of many.* Sure, it's been done before, but there is something empowering about being surrounded by a group of peers who stand, raise their arms or come forward together as a sign of their commitment to be kind to the less popular kids at school, to avoid pornography on the Internet or to share their faith even when it's difficult. Because of the powerful influence of positive peer pressure, we've given you all sorts of closing, rousing, group-bonding acts of commitment to help you form a group of young believers who, though limping at times, march forward together!

Kara Powell
Director of the Center for Youth and Family Ministry
Assistant Professor of Youth, Family and Culture
Fuller Theological Seminary

STANDING FIRM

THE BIG IDEA

Standing firm under small pressures gives us the ability to stand firm under the big ones.

SESSION AIMS

In this session you will guide students to (1) learn that success is found in daily small things—not just in big things; (2) feel the importance of obeying God's Word in small ways in their everyday lives; and (3) identify specific small areas where they need to stand against peer pressure this week.

THE BIGGEST VERSE

"Whoever can be trusted with very little can also be trusted with much, and whoever is dishonest with very little will also be dishonest with much" (Luke 16:10).

OTHER IMPORTANT VERSES

1 Samuel 16:7; Daniel 1:1-21; 3:1-30; Zechariah 4:10; Luke 19:11-27; 1 Peter 2:11-12

Note: Additional options and worksheets in 8¹/₂" x 11" format for this session are available for download at **www.gospellight.com/uncommon/jh_friends_and_peer_pressure.zip**.

STARTER

Option 1: The Missing Ingredient. For this option, you need a whiteboard, a dry-erase marker, a large serving tray, frosting (ready-made is fine) and home-made cupcakes (see recipe below).

Ahead of time, use the recipe below to prepare two batches of cupcakes (get one or more of your students to help you if you can), but *leave out* the baking powder in one of the batches. The batch missing this small but vital ingredient will be very flat (which should make it fairly easy to keep the batches separated) and not quite as tasty!

4 tbsp. butter	1 cup flour
$1/2$ cup sugar	1 tsp. baking powder
1 egg	$1/3$ cup milk
$1/2$ tsp. vanilla	cupcake papers

Preheat oven to 350° F. Cream butter and sugar together in a mixing bowl. Add vanilla and beat in eggs, mixing thoroughly. In a separate bowl, mix flour and baking powder (except in second batch, where you will skip the baking powder). Gently mix flour mixture into butter mixture. Add milk and mix. Put cupcake papers into a muffin tin. Fill each cup two-thirds full of batter. Bake for 15 to 20 minutes, until a toothpick inserted in the middle comes out clean. Take cupcakes out of the muffin tins to cool, and then frost as desired. Makes about 6 cupcakes.

Greet students and bring out the tray of cupcakes without pointing out why some are flatter than others. If you have brave students, invite them to taste one cupcake from each batch; then write out the ingredients as listed above on the whiteboard. Then ask the following questions:

Youth Leader Tip

Peer influence and the pressure to conform can be felt most strongly when students are grappling with the question, *Do I really matter?* More often than not, they will search for answers in any place other than the one where they can find lasting significance—in a relationship with Jesus.[1]

- What's the difference between the two batches of cupcakes? *One is flat and tastes kind of funny.* Explain that the difference between them is that one batch is missing an ingredient from the recipe.
- What is the missing ingredient? *Baking powder.*
- How can such a small ingredient make such a big difference in a recipe? *The baking powder has the most impact, even though it's one of the smallest amounts needed for the recipe.*
- Can you think of any other examples where what seems to be a small ingredient or part is vital for the whole thing to work? *Parts in a car engine; a member of a sports team; the heart in the human body; the ripcord on a parachute; and so on.*

Transition by explaining that you're starting a new series today on peer pressure and, as you'll see, the small decisions we make when we're around others can have a big impact on our lives—and theirs.

Option 2: Tidal Wave. For this option, you need an adult volunteer to referee, candy for prizes, and one small unbreakable object for every student, something that can be passed from one person to another during the game.

Greet students and have them form a circle. Distribute an object to each student and instruct students to begin passing objects to their right when you give the signal. If an object is dropped, the student who dropped it will be escorted out of the circle by the referee, but the object will continue to be passed around. *Note:* You can make the game even livelier by yelling out "Reverse direction!" periodically so that players must pass objects the opposite way (and drop them in the process!).

Eventually, the objects being passed around will far outnumber the students still in the game. Signal to stop when two players are left; award them the candy prizes and explain that, as you start a new series on peer pressure today, you'll see that the better we get at standing firm against smaller waves of pressure, the better we'll be at standing firm against the bigger tidal waves that are sure to come.

MESSAGE

Option 1: *Rack, Shack and Benny*. You'll need several Bibles, a TV, a DVD player, a copy of the Veggie Tales movie *Rack, Shack and Benny*, a whiteboard and a dry-erase marker.

Ahead of time, cue the movie approximately eight minutes from the beginning to the 10-minute scene in which Bob, Larry and Junior refuse to eat too much chocolate.

Distribute Bibles and ask several volunteers to take turns reading through Daniel 3:1-30; then explain that you're going to show a reenactment of the story, well, vegetable style! Show the clip, and then discuss the following:

- What was Junior's (Shack's) reason for not participating in the chocolate feast? *His mom told him too much candy was bad for him.*
- How did Junior convince Bob and Larry not to eat too many chocolate bunnies? *By reminding them that they should obey their parents even when their parents aren't around.*

Ask students to share examples of times when they've heard the phrase "everybody's doing it" and how they responded when they heard it, and then continue:

- When Nebbie K. Nezzar asked Bob, Larry and Junior to bow down before the bunny, did you notice any difference in Bob and Larry's behavior? *Bob and Larry didn't have to be convinced by Junior not to sing the song; they already knew what they believed and weren't willing to compromise.*
- How did the chocolate-eating experience prepare Bob, Larry and Junior for this new challenge? *It gave them confidence to stand up for their beliefs and what their moms taught them, no matter what the cost.*
- What things does the movie have in common with Daniel 3:1-30? Write responses on the whiteboard (students should be able to come up with a long list).

Ask a volunteer to read Daniel 1:1-21, and then discuss how Shadrach, Meshach and Abednego's decision prepared them for the furnace test that was to come. (It almost certainly prepared them to face this bigger challenge to their faith.)

Option 2: Size Doesn't Matter. For this option, you need several Bibles, a large-currency bill ($100) and several quarters. If it's tough to scrounge up a $100 bill on a youth-worker's salary, write a check for that amount and make sure it gets ripped up afterward.

Explain that often people think bigger is better. For example, it used to be that you could buy a small-sized soda in a convenience store or at the movies; now you can only buy soda in big cups. In fact, McDonald's doesn't even sell small sodas anymore—the smallest size it sells is a "regular." Same thing with Starbuck's coffee—its small is called a "tall."

In God's eyes, however, size doesn't matter—not physical size or social status. Read Daniel 3:1-30 and explain that small things (a.k.a. *unimportant* things) are pretty important to God.

Compared to the king, Shadrach, Meshach and Abednego were pretty small and unimportant—yet their impact on the king was huge.

Invite an adult and one of the shorter students to come forward to act as visual aids as you illustrate that size, age or prestige makes little difference to God: When Samuel was told to go and anoint David king over Israel, old Sammy was pretty impressed by the size of David's brothers (walk over to the adult). But God said to him about David's brother Eliab, "Do not consider his appearance or his height, for I have rejected him. The LORD does not look at the things man looks at. Man looks at the outward appearance, but the LORD looks at the heart" (1 Samuel 16:7). To God, it's the condition of our hearts that matters, not the condition of our bodies; this means that no matter how young or small—no matter how insignificant we seem—God can still work through our decisions, even the small ones.

Note: When an activity suggests bringing students forward based upon a certain physical characteristic, do not select students who may be adversely affected by having their differences pointed out.

Explain that sometimes we can become discouraged when we have to start small with something that we desperately want to be great at. Share an example of an experience from your life where you had to learn a skill and were frustrated by not being good at it immediately. Then continue by explaining that those times are sometimes the most important times, because often, that's when big things start. Share the following illustration from a plaque marking the birthplace of Abraham Lincoln near Hodgenville, Kentucky:

"Any news down t' the village, Ezry?"

"Well, Squire McLains's gone t' Washington t' see Madison swore in, and ol' Spellman tells me this Bonaparte fella has captured most o' Spain. What's new out here, neighbor?"

"Nuthin', nuthin' a'tall, 'cept fer a new baby born t' Tom Lincoln's. Nothin' ever happens out here."

Ask the group who the men were talking about. (*Abraham Lincoln.*) Point out that these guys thought that nothing important ever happened in their town, but one of the greatest American presidents was born there. It was a small beginning of a great life.

Ask a volunteer to read Daniel 1:1-21; then point out that when Shadrach, Meshach and Abednego refused to eat the meat that the king offered them, it probably seemed like a small thing, but it paved the way for the bigger challenges they would face later. In fact, if they hadn't resisted the pressure to eat the king's food, they probably wouldn't have been able to resist the pressure to bow down to the king's statue when their lives were at stake.[2] The same thing is true for us—resisting the small pressures in our lives gives us the ability to resist bigger ones.

Explain that for Shadrach, Meshach and Abednego it was the simpler action of refusing to eat the defiled meat that almost certainly prepared them for even bigger challenges to come. The same is true in our lives. It's those small actions that will determine who we are and what we do when the big pressures come. It's how we respond when classmates are giving the substitute teacher a hard time or what we say when friends are mocking the new kid's weird outfit—these small things prepare us for bigger challenges that come later on.

DIG

Option 1: Practice Makes Good. For this option, you need unlined 3x5-inch index cards and pens or pencils.

Distribute index cards and pens or pencils and instruct students to draw a picture of themselves doing something that they are good at (e.g., playing an instrument, skateboarding, reading). Explain that it must be something they had to practice doing to become good at. Allow three minutes or so; then ask several to share about what they drew. Discuss the following:

Youth Leader Tip

When leading a discussion, consider yourself part of the group. Participate in answering the questions rather than just asking them. Create an atmosphere or honesty and vulnerability by giving your own response to difficult questions first.

- Is the thing you're good at easy or hard to do? *It may be easy for the student but it still may be hard for other people to do.*
- Was it always hard (or easy)? *Most things are hard to do when you first start doing them; they become easier with practice.*
- How did you become good at doing this? *Practice; spending lots of time at it.*
- Did you enjoy all the times that you had to practice? *Chances are that no one enjoys practicing something every single time they have to do it!*
- How does someone become a better Christian? *Practice, practice, practice!*
- How can you practice being a Christian? *By disciplining yourself to do those little things you don't want to do, such as reading the Bible, praying, fasting, tithing, and so forth.*
- How does practice relate to peer pressure? *The more you're in the habit of saying no when everyone is saying yes (or vice versa), the better at it you'll become.*

Option 2: A Guy Named Tiger. For this option, you need just the info below. Share the following information about a famous golfer:

- His first name is Eldrick.
- His dad taught him every day about all aspects of the game—driving, chipping, putting.
- He knew the difference between a par 5, a par 4 and a par 3 at the age of 18 months.
- He was so talented, he demonstrated his golf skills on TV when only a toddler.
- He shot a 48 for nine holes at age three.
- He won his first Under-10 tournament at age four.
- He beat his dad for the first time on a par-3 course at age eight.
- He beat his dad no-holds-barred at age 11.
- He was the youngest player ever to win the U.S. Junior Amateur Championship (at 15) and won it two more times at 16 and 17.
- At the age of 18, he was the youngest player ever to win the U.S. Amateur Championship, and he won it two more times at the ages of 19 and 20.
- He was the youngest player ever to win The Masters (at 21) and set a Masters' record with a 12-stroke victory margin.

- He set a P.G.A. record, winning six tournaments in a row in the 1999-2000 season.
- His nickname? Tiger!

Discuss the following:

- How did Tiger Woods become such an outstanding golfer? *He had lots of raw talent, but it was his (and his father's) dedication to practice that made him great.*
- Do you think Tiger enjoyed all the days he went out to practice golf? *Even though he loved his sport, there were probably times when he had to push himself to practice.*
- What would it take for you to become an excellent athlete or musician or salesperson or teacher? *Dedication, practice, discipline.*
- If someone really wanted to be like Jesus, what would it take to become more like Him? *Dedication, discipline, practice.*
- How does practice relate to peer pressure? *The more you're in the habit of saying no when everyone is saying yes (or, for that matter, yes when everyone is saying no), the better at it you'll become.*

APPLY

Option 1: Walk the Talk. For this option, you need paper, copies of "Walk the Talk" (found on the following two pages) and pens or pencils.

Distribute "Walk the Talk" and pens or pencils. Explain that the items on this list are spiritual disciplines. They're *spiritual* because they help us grow closer to God, and *disciplines* because sometimes we have to push ourselves to do them. Emphasize that these disciplines are not an end in themselves; they are ways to train us to become more like Christ. *Note:* The handout is not an exhaustive list of spiritual disciplines—it's simply a good foundation for students to build on.

Ask students to identify from the list one or two areas in their lives that they would like to change and then fill in the blanks for those areas. Allow a few minutes for students to complete the handout; then instruct them to write the name of a mature Christian they would like to have as a mentor for the next month—someone they feel comfortable discussing their need for spiritual discipline with. The mentors will keep in touch with the students, encouraging and holding them accountable for their spiritual discipline. Encourage students

WALK THE TALK

All good athletes know that they have to have a training regimen in order to keep their bodies in top shape to excel at their sport. We also need to have a training regimen in order to become more like Christ. We won't ever become better Christians just by sliding into discipleship; we must put ourselves into training. Look through the list below and choose specific areas where you want to go into training. Make sure you clarify how long you want to be committed to that training.

PRAYER

Talking with God, setting aside specific times in our day to praise and thank Him, confessing our sins and bringing requests to Him

I commit to pray for _____ (how long) at

_____ (what time) every day for the next

_____ (period of time).

BIBLE STUDY

Reading the Bible, reading devotionals or other books to help us understand the Bible, meditating (thinking) about what the Bible says

I commit to study the Bible for _____ (how long)

at _____ (what time) every day for the next

_____ (period of time).

SOLITUDE AND SILENCE

Spending extended periods of time alone to listen to God

I commit to be in solitude and silence for _____ (how long) at

_____ (what time) every day for the next _____

(period of time).

FASTING

Going without food for a meal, a day or more than one day (clear this with your parents before you do this one), giving up other things (TV, movies, gum, sleeping in) for a period of time

I commit to fast from _____ (what) at _____

(how long) for the next _____ (period of time).

TITHING

Giving money to the church or other Christian work

I commit to give _____ (how much) to _____

(where) for the next _____ (period of time).

HUMiLiTY

Not bragging about yourself, but considering others better than yourself

One way that I will practice humility is to _____

(specific action) for the next _____ (period of time).

SERViCe

Serving others through acts of kindness or mercy

One way that I will serve others will be to _____

(action) for the next _____ (period of time).

Someone who can coach me through this and show me what to do, both by example and

encouragement, is _____ (name of person).

to think of someone besides you; however, offer yourself as an alternative mentor if students can't think of anyone else. Don't alienate students by discounting your own importance in their spiritual journey!

Invite anyone who would like to share what they wrote to do so; then take a few moments to ask students who they chose as their mentors for the week. Write down the mentors' names and offer to contact them with the requests if students would like for you to. Close in prayer, thanking God for providing ways for us to become stronger, better Christians and asking Him to help students to become spiritually disciplined in a way they can see during the next month.

Option 2: Sharing Our Faith in Small Ways. You'll need a copy of "Sharing Our Faith in Small Ways" (found on the next page) for every three students and pens or pencils.

Divide students into groups of three and distribute one copy of "Sharing Our Faith in Small Ways" and pens or pencils to each group. Instruct students to work within their groups to come up with one small but difficult peer pressure situation involving friends in each of the four categories on the handout. Allow a few minutes for groups to work; then have the groups exchange papers and ask them to come up with responses to the situations on the papers they exchanged.

Allow more time for students to respond; then have students return the handouts to their original groups. Invite volunteers to share the situations and the responses. Challenge students to commit to doing one or more of the items suggested.

Close in prayer, thanking God for the opportunities He gives us to share our faith and asking Him to help students keep their commitments in the coming weeks.

SHARING OUR FAITH IN SMALL WAYS

Here are four different places where junior-highers can face peer pressure. Write a small area of temptation in each situation. For example, you might write "My friends make fun of Coach behind her back" in the class section or "My best friend is really disrespectful to his mom when I'm over there" in the weekend section.

IN CLASS

AT LUNCH

AFTER SCHOOL

DURING WEEKENDS/ FREE TIME

REFLECT

The following short devotions are for the students to reflect on and answer during the week. You can make a copy of these pages and distribute to your class or print out from the PDF available online at **www.gospellight.com/un common/uncommon_jh_friends_and_peer_pressure.zip**.

1—STAND STRONG

Hey, head over to 1 Peter 5:6-11.

How much would you pay to be the strongest person at your school? Probably a lot, especially if you're a guy who wants to impress that new girl in your math class. Well, if you want to get real strength, check out 1 Peter 5:6-11.

In verses 6 through 9, each verse has one command (something that we should do) and one reason why we should obey that command. Fill in the following two columns (the first one is done for you):

COMMAND   WHY?

v. 6: Humble yourselves   God will lift you up

v. 7: _____   _____

v. 8: _____   _____

v. 9: _____   _____

What does verse 10 say is the ultimate result of obeying these commands?

_____
_____
_____
_____
_____

Which of the verses do you find most helpful when you think about your struggle to stand under peer pressure? Why?

_____
_____
_____
_____

Memorize that verse! Like, right now!

2—SMALL THINGS

Find Ecclesiastes 12:13. If you're a little lost, it comes after Psalms and Proverbs.
We all want to do big and important things, don't we? Really, who wants to do things that don't seem important, like making your bed or setting the table or doing homework? We'd rather do the big and important things that get others' attention and make a difference in the world, right?

According to Ecclesiastes 12:13, what is our job as creatures made by God? Does this seem big and important to you?

_____

_____

_____

_____

_____

_____

Write down five things that you will do this week that may not feel very important but that are important according to this verse.

_____

_____

_____

_____

_____

3—RIGHT RELATIONSHIPS

If you want to see how the Bible describes a TV show, flip on over to Proverbs 2:12-19.
TV makes dating and romance seem pretty easy. Guy meets girl. Guy falls in love with girl. Guy sleeps with girl. Guy and girl are happy.
But what TV doesn't show you is some of the consequences of guy-sleeps-with-girl. Things like disease, heartbreak and feelings of emptiness, self-doubt and betrayal. And that's because the guy and the girl don't follow the Bible's plan for dating. They give in to pressures, both their own desires and the messages of our culture, and plunge in too deeply.

You may not be dating right now, but some day soon you probably will be. What kind of relationships do you want to have?

_____

_____

_____

_____

_____

What kind of pressures will you give in to?

_____

_____

_____

_____

Which ones will you stand against?

_____

_____

_____

_____

Ask God right to give you strength so that all of your relationships, including those with the opposite gender, are just like He would want them to be.

4—WHEN YOU FALL, GET BACK UP!

Check out Acts 15:36-40. What happens when we fail? What happens when pressure comes and we give in to the pressure instead of doing what is right?

The good news is that everyone fails. Even the early followers of Jesus gave in to pressure at times! According to this passage from Acts, why didn't Paul want to take John Mark with him on his journey?

- ❏ He thought he dressed like a geek.
- ❏ His luggage didn't match.
- ❏ He had wimped out and deserted them before.
- ❏ His name was too confusing.

Later though, Scripture shows that John Mark regained Paul's trust (see Colossians 4:10) and even became an important part of Paul's ministry (see 2 Timothy 4:11).

Have you ever given in to temptations or fallen under pressure? Who hasn't?! The good news is that when we fail, God wants to restore us, or bring us back into a place of strength under pressure! Take a moment and ask God for His forgiveness during a time that you failed.

Is there someone else you need to apologize to? Or maybe someone else needs to know you forgive him or her. Remember the example of John Mark and Paul as you try to live your life standing firm under pressure.

BEWARE AND BE WISE

THE BIG IDEA

It's easier to resist peer pressure if you don't willingly put yourself in situations where you'll face it.

SESSION AIMS

In this session you will guide students to (1) learn how to discern which tempting situations to avoid; (2) feel brave enough to walk away from negative situations; and (3) act by walking away from challenging negative peer pressure situations they're bound to face soon.

THE BIGGEST VERSE

"And though she spoke to Joseph day after day, he refused to go to bed with her or even be with her" (Genesis 39:10).

OTHER IMPORTANT VERSES

Genesis 39:1-23; 40–50; Joshua 1:6; Proverbs 1:10-16; 4:10-15; 5:8; 26:11; 1 Corinthians 6:18; 10:13; 1 Thessalonians 5:22-24; 1 Timothy 6:11; 2 Timothy 2:22

Note: Additional options and worksheets in 8½" x 11" format for this session are available for download at **www.gospellight.com/uncommon/jh_friends_and_peer_pressure.zip**.

STARTER

Option 1: The Three Stooges. For this option, you need a chair for every student and one for yourself.

Greet students and explain they're going to play a memory game. Instruct them to move their chairs into a large circle (if the group is larger than 25 students, have them form more than one circle). Stand in the middle of the circle and explain the rules of the game: You're going to point at a student and name one of the original Three Stooges (Moe, Curly or Larry). If you name Moe, the student must state his or her name; if you name Larry, the student must name the person to his or her left; and if you name Curly, the student must name the person to his or her right. (Got it? Great, because we're totally confused now!)

If the student responds with the correct information before you can count to 10 as quickly as possible, he or she avoids having to switch seats with anyone—yet. If the student doesn't respond correctly before you can count to 10, he or she must trade seats with you. Trading seats for incorrect answers will ensure that students constantly have to remember new names!

After a few minutes of playing the game, stop and remind students that there were two Stooges that came after Curly: Shemp and Curly Joe. These names are now going to be added to the game. The same rules as before apply, but now when you name Shemp, the student you point to must name the person two seats to his or her left; if you name Curly Joe, the student must name the person two seats to his or her right. Whew!

Explain that the Three Stooges were willing to do things that no one in their right mind would do. That's what made them so funny and popular. Unlike us, though, they were acting goofy because that was their profession. Sometimes we find ourselves in circumstances in real life where we do things we normally wouldn't do. Oftentimes, those circumstances revolve around a group of people who are doing something that tempts us to go along with the crowd. Today we're going to look at some of the choices we make and the situations where we're more likely to do things we normally wouldn't.

Option 2: Cotton-Ball Relay. For this option, you need two folding tables, four broiler pans (or heavy-duty cookie sheets), a stopwatch (or a watch with a seconds indicator), lots of cotton balls, some tissues or napkins for cleaning up, a jar of petroleum jelly and a prize for the winning team.

Ahead of time, set up the tables at opposite ends of the room and fill two of the broiler pans with cotton balls. Set the pans with the cotton balls on one table and the empty pans on the other.

Greet students and divide them into six teams. Ask each team to select a team representative to come forward. Once all six reps have come forward, explain that the teams are going to compete to see who can get the most cotton balls from one end of the room to the other. Yes, of course there's a catch: Contestants cannot use any body part except their noses to pick up and move the cotton balls!

Have two of the team reps step up to begin the game. Assign each rep one of the empty pans at the other end of the room, then smear petroleum jelly on their noses and signal the start. Allow exactly three minutes, then stop the game, count the cotton balls transferred by each team and set up for the next two team reps. Continue this until all six reps have competed. Announce the winning team's total; award that team its prizes.

Transition to the next step by asking the team reps if they felt foolish trying to move the cotton balls with petroleum jelly all over their noses. Explain that we all put ourselves in foolish situations once in a while. Sometimes that's okay, but sometimes it can be really dangerous—especially when it comes to giving in to peer pressure or temptation. Right now you're going to find out that it's best to stay away from tempting situations when we can.

MESSAGE

Option 1: Go Ahead, Make Me Smile. For this option, you need three prizes (gift certificates for ice cream, pizza or the next junior-high event) and a stopwatch (or a watch with a seconds indicator).

Ask for someone (the Tempter) who thinks he or she can get anyone to laugh and then ask for three Temptees who think that no one can get them to laugh. Explain that they will be playing "Go Ahead, Make Me Smile." The Tempter will be given 30 seconds to make each of the Temptees smile. Give a prize to the Tempter if he/she is successful in making someone smile or to the Temptees who are able to resist the urge to smile.

Transition by explaining that Genesis 39 tells about a more serious temptation. Briefly familiarize students with the betrayal of Joseph by his brothers that eventually led to Joseph's predicament with Potiphar's wife.[1] Ask them to imagine being Joseph. Say, "You've been sold by your brothers and now you serve an Egyptian master. Yet Genesis 39:2-6 repeatedly mentions how God was with Joseph. What does that tell you about God?" Allow for responses; then continue by saying, "It might surprise you to find out that God is always with us, even when our circumstances seem to be going down the tubes."

Discuss the following:

- Why wouldn't Joseph give in to Potiphar's wife? *Because he knew that it would be a sin against God and against his boss.*
- What was Joseph's strategy to resist the pressure placed upon him by Potiphar's wife? *He refused to even be near her (see Genesis 39:10).*
- Was it a good strategy? *It worked as long as he wasn't near her.*
- Why did Potiphar's wife claim that Joseph attacked her? *She was probably embarrassed and angered by his rebuff and decided to get revenge on Joseph for refusing her.*

Explain that Joseph was no fool. He knew that the closer he got to the fiery temptation of Potiphar's wife, the more likely he was to get burned by it. Although he ended up in jail anyway, it was his refusal to give in to the temptation to sin that eventually led to God opening doors for him to leave the jail and serve the pharaoh in ways that saved not only Egypt, but also much of Israel, including his own family (see Genesis 40–50). God honored Joseph's obedience to Him—maybe not in Joseph's preferred time, but in God's own perfect timing.

Option 2: Go the Other Way. For this option, you need several Bibles.

Ask students to share what their favorite food is; then ask if any of them have ever tried to give up their favorite food due to fasting, allergies or a diet. Allow for responses; then share the following story:

Kyle decided he wanted to lose some weight, so he made up his mind to go on a diet. The first day was really hard, especially during lunchtime when it seemed that everyone was enjoying huge sandwiches, chips and cookies—and all Kyle had was a plain salad.

Youth Leader Tip

Never underestimate the insecurity of junior-high students! Despite all their talk and bravado, they are often still scared children on the inside. Look for ways to verbally build them up in whatever ways you can. The results will be amazing.

One afternoon, two days into his diet, Kyle got on his skateboard and skated his way over to the mall right past the ice cream parlor. Ooh, it smelled so good! He stopped, turned around, marched right in and ordered a banana split. The clerk brought the banana split to Kyle's table, and Kyle picked up the spoon and . . .

Ask, "What do you think happened next? Did Kyle eat the ice cream or stick to his diet?" Allow for responses, and then point out that it was a really bad idea for Kyle to go into the ice cream parlor; it was probably not even a good idea for him to skate by the ice cream parlor so that he would be tempted to go in. If he really wanted to stick to his diet, he would have been better off to be aware of the temptation and avoid it. Discuss the following:

- Some people are literally addicted to food. What other things can people be addicted to? *Alcohol, work, gambling, TV, video games, sex, to name just a few.*

- How can an addict kick his or her habit? *Stay away from situations that would tempt him or her; get help from other people to not give in.*

Distribute Bibles and ask a volunteer to read Proverbs 26:11. Explain that even though it's pretty gross, it's true—someone who's addicted to something will have a really hard time staying away from his or her addiction. Ask another volunteer to read 1 Thessalonians 5:22-24. Explain that instead of putting ourselves in situations where we might be tempted, we should avoid them and turn our focus to God and His promise to be with us and help us resist the temptation to sin.

DIG

Option 1: I Never. For this option, you need two large bags of M&Ms (or a similar candy).

Divide students into groups of 8 to 10 and distribute 10 pieces of candy to each student. No eating the candy yet! Explain that groups are going to play "I Never." Here's how to play: In each group, students take turns saying something they've never done or some place they have never been (e.g., "I've never shaved my legs" or "I've never been to Florida"). Anyone in the group who has done that thing or been to that place must give one piece of candy to the student who hasn't.

Allow several minutes for students to play; then regroup and discuss: "When someone has done something, he or she has gained experience. Is it better at your school to be experienced or inexperienced?" (Get ready—here come the giggles and answers about sex. Be prepared to keep the situation under control.)

- In what situations would it be good to be able to say "I never did that"? *Drinking, drugs, sex, stealing, and so forth.*

- How can we know which situations we should avoid? *The Bible gives guidelines; parents, teachers, and other authority figures set rules to follow and advise us; more mature Christians can give good advice; seeing how certain behaviors destroy lives.*

Option 2: Not Okay. For this option, you will need a whiteboard and a dry-erase marker.

Share the following case study:

Ashley was 14 years old. One night at youth group, the youth pastor talked about God's plan for sex to be saved for marriage. She made a commitment that night to stay pure until her wedding night.

Since Ashley's boyfriend, Nate, was 16 and wasn't a churchgoer, Ashley's parents weren't thrilled with their relationship. Because they trusted Ashley, they gave in and allowed her to see Nate—but only if they went out with a group of people.

One Friday night, Ashley and Nate made arrangements to meet at the movies with a group of friends. Nate's parents had let him borrow the car, and after the movie, Nate invited Ashley to go cruising. Her parents were expecting her to go out for pizza with the group after the movie, but she agreed to go with Nate anyway, reasoning that they would wind up at the pizza parlor after they drove around a little.

Nate drove around and they eventually wound up in the park. Nate turned off the car and leaned over to kiss Ashley. He whispered, "Why don't we get in the back seat where we'll be more comfortable?"

Divide students into groups of five to seven and instruct the groups to discuss what Ashley should do. Allow three to five minutes for group discussion; then regroup and ask groups to share the advice they came up with. Discuss the following: "Nate was the one putting the pressure on Ashley, but what mistakes did Ashley make in this situation?" (She was wrong to go cruising with Nate when she knew her parents expected her to stay with the group; she was wrong to disobey her parents. You might point out that her first mistake might have been dating a non-Christian in the first place.)

Draw three columns on the whiteboard and ask students to come up with a list of similar peer pressure situations. (Examples might include going to a party where people are drinking, hanging around with people who shoplift, getting involved in a gang.) Write their answers in the left column.

Label the other two columns "Okay" and "Not Okay." Have students vote with a show of hands whether or not it's okay for a Christian to be in each situation and tally up the votes in each column. Ask students to defend their votes in each situation. Explain that Christians are not safe from temptation or peer pressure just because they hang out only with other Christians. What's important is to think about the situations we place ourselves in and be aware of our vulnerability to temptations.

APPLY

Option 1: Role-Play. For this option, you need copies of "Role-Play" (found on the following page). Ahead of time, cut the handouts into individual role-play scenarios.

Explain that peer pressure situations almost always have "pressure lines"—things that people say to really put the pressure on. One of the best ways to walk away from these situations is to come up with a good response to the pressure line. For example, a pressure line might be, "Come on, everybody's doing it." Your response could be, "Not everybody's doing it, because I'm not!"

Divide students into groups of three to five and give each group a different role-play scenario. Let groups know that they have two minutes to come up with a role-play that ends with the person who's being pressured responding with a counter to the pressure line and walking away without giving in to the pressure. (All students in each group must participate in the role-play.) Allow two minutes for preparation; then have groups take turns acting out their role-plays.

Close in prayer, thanking God for giving us the courage and strength to resist temptation and the discernment to recognize some risky situations. Ask Him to help students know just what to say in order to walk away from tempting peer pressure situations.

Role-Play

Role-Play 1: You're at a friend's house on a Friday night. Your friend's older brother and his friends come in with some beer. They offer some to you, saying, "Come on, try it. It'll make you loosen up a little and have more fun."

How do you respond to this pressure line?

_____

_____

_____

_____

Role-Play 2: You and your friends are at a convenience store after school. Your friends come up with a plan for someone to distract the clerk so that everyone else can steal stuff. "Oh, come on," they plead with you. "That's why the prices are so high; they expect us to steal things. Besides, it's not like it's a car or something."

How do you respond to this pressure line?

_____

_____

_____

_____

Role-Play 3: A really popular guy in class whispers for you to show him your answers to the big test. "I'm too busy to study," he whispers. "I'll study next time. Be a pal!"

How do you respond to this pressure line?

_____

_____

_____

Role-Play 4: You're at your friend's house when she gets a phone call from some good-looking guy who's at a home alone. He's got a couple of friends over and invites you and your friend too. Your friend wants to go, but you told your parents you'd be at your friend's house all evening. "Let's go for a little while," she says. "Your folks won't even know we left."

How do you respond to this pressure line?

_____

_____

_____

_____

_____

Option 2: *The Wizard of Oz.* You'll need a TV, a DVD player, a copy of the classic movie *The Wizard of Oz*, copies of "Courage Medals" (found on the next
page) and pens or pencils. *Option:* Copy the handout onto cardstock.

Ahead of time, cue the film approximately 49 minutes from the beginning
to the scene where Dorothy meets the Cowardly Lion. *Note:* You'll be showing
two clips from the video—the first ends when the characters head down the
Yellow Brick Road; the second begins another 37 minutes into the video (an
hour and 31 minutes from the beginning) where the Wizard gives the Cowardly
Lion a medal. Also, cut the handouts into individual medals.

Show both clips, and then explain that when Dorothy, the Scarecrow, the
Tin Man and the Cowardly Lion finally meet the Wizard, the Lion learns that he
has always had courage; he just lacked a medal. Just like the Lion, you already
have courage. You have the courage to walk away from negative peer pressure.

Distribute medals and pens or pencils and invite students to draw a symbol
or picture in the middle of their medals representing a negative peer pressure
situation they might need the courage to walk away from. (For example, someone may draw a cigarette if he or she is being pressured to smoke, or a test if
he or she is being pressured to cheat.)

Ask volunteers to share what they've drawn. Give each one who shares a
personal word of affirmation about how courageous he or she is. Encourage students to carry their medals with them this week to remind them to have the
courage to avoid giving in to peer pressure.

Youth Leader Tip

As youth workers, we are dealing with students
who are in need of decision-making skills and
discernment. We can help them navigate their
decisions with godly discernment and wisdom.[2]

COURAGE MEDALS

REFLECT

The following short devotions are for the students to reflect on and answer during the week. You can make a copy of these pages and distribute to your class or print out from the PDF available online at **www.gospellight.com/un common/uncommon_jh_friends_and_peer_pressure.zip.**

1—CHOICES

Walk on over to Proverbs 4:25-27.

Joey is confused: "In this proverb, is God actually telling us not to go hiking in the mountains or walking along the beach because we should only make level paths for our feet and take ways that are firm?" He continues, "I mean, how can I ever get anywhere if I can't turn right or left?"

"No, no, no," you begin, trying to calm poor Joey down. "This proverb isn't about actually walking down the street. It is about the choices we make in life. God loves us and wants us to stay away from bad situations. God wants us to stay safe, so He uses the picture of walking to help us understand that. I mean, when you walk on ground that isn't even, after a while you'll probably fall and hurt yourself. In the same way, if we don't make wise choices, we can get hurt—or we'll end up going the wrong direction and getting lost!"

Joey is so lucky to have a wise friend like you!

Rewrite this proverb in a way that Joey (and maybe some of your friends) can understand it better.

_____
_____
_____
_____
_____
_____

How can you walk straight ahead today?

_____
_____
_____
_____
_____

2—GOD WANTS TO GET YOUR ATTENTION

Run over to Jonah 1:1-5,12-17; 2:10 and 3:1-3.

Wow. There's a lot to the story of Jonah, but from the small sections that you have just read, what was Jonah trying to do? He was trying to run away from God! What two things did God send to let Jonah know that he was going the wrong way?

❒   An email and a balloon-a-gram
❒   A storm and a huge fish
❒   Charlie's Angels and James Bond
❒   The school cafeteria lady and the school security cop

God still works today! In the past, you have probably gotten into situations that were bad. Can you think of ways that God tried to redirect you? (Hopefully not through a large fish, but maybe through friends or Bible verses or songs that came to your mind at just the right moment.)

_____

_____

_____

_____

_____

_____

_____

_____

What ways might you expect God to warn you when you're tempted to do something you shouldn't do?

_____

_____

_____

_____

_____

_____

_____

Spend some time thanking God for working on you!

3—OFF WITH HIS HEAD

Dig into Mark 6:21-28.

Okay, gross! And bad! Now, before King Herod did the awful thing you just read about, he felt distressed (verse 26). In other words, he didn't actually want to follow through on what was asked of him—but he did it anyway! Why did he do it?

❒   He didn't want to look lame in front of his guests.
❒   He wanted to gross out his guests.
❒   His guests were getting bored and he wanted to liven up his party.

The things we say or promise to do can get us into trouble! Herod chose to do the wrong thing because he swore a promise in front of a crowd of important people he wanted to impress. In the same way, we sometimes talk our way into bad situations—especially when we are talking to people we are trying to impress.

What are two ways you can keep yourself from talking your way into bad situations? (It could be a single word you say to yourself to hold you back, such as "Herod," or it could be a friend who will warn you!) Write those two ways down.

_____

_____

_____

_____

_____

4—DON'T JUMP!

Check out John 6:14-15—like, pronto.

Isn't that interesting? Even Jesus had to avoid certain situations at times! The funny thing is that some situations look good on the outside but aren't so good when you look deeper into them. These are some of the hardest situations to avoid! For instance, don't you want to ask Jesus what is wrong with being a king? Well, we know that Jesus will reign on earth as King someday—but it will happen when God the Father puts Jesus on the throne and not because people tried to force it.

Have you ever been in this kind of situation, one that looks good at first but really isn't good? What was attractive about that situation at first?

_____

_____

_____

_____

_____

_____

Whatever it was, when and how did you discover that the situation that looked good really wasn't so good?

_____

_____

_____

_____

_____

_____

Ask God to give you wisdom and insight so that in future situations you will not jump into things that only look good on the outside but are not good when you look deeper into them.

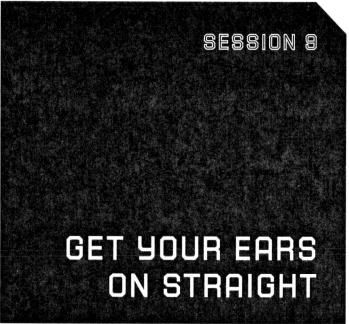

GET YOUR EARS ON STRAIGHT

THE BIG IDEA

Negative peer pressure loses its punch if we know who to listen to and who to ignore.

SESSION AIMS

In this session you will guide students to (1) learn to discern who they should listen to; (2) feel a sense of unity with other students in establishing high standards of behavior; and (3) covenant as a group to encourage godly behavior in the future.

THE BIGGEST VERSE

"But Rehoboam rejected the advice the elders gave him and consulted the young men who had grown up with him and were serving him" (1 Kings 12:8).

OTHER IMPORTANT VERSES

1 Kings 11:9-13; 12:1-20; Proverbs 2:3-6; 3:5-6; Acts 15:32; Hebrews 3:12-13; 10:24; Titus 2:6-7; James 1:5

Note: Additional options and worksheets in 8$^1/_2$" x 11" format for this session are available for download at **www.gospellight.com/uncommon/jh_friends_and_peer_pressure.zip**.

STARTER

Option 1: Sardines. For this option, you need a large meeting space—ideally multiple rooms (or outside spaces) with small hiding places.

Greet students and explain that you're going to start this session with a variation of Hide-and-Seek called "Sardines." It's actually the reverse of the original game; in Sardines, one person hides and the rest seek! When a seeker finds the person hiding, instead of yelling out the discovery, the seeker hides with him or her in that same space. This continues, with the seekers becoming hiders until a large group of people is crammed inside a small hiding place.

Play a few rounds, and then bring everyone back together and explain that this game is interesting because it sometimes takes a long time to find the first person, but as the number of people hiding in one area grows, it becomes pretty obvious where they are hiding. Groups are noticeable, and the bigger the group, the more noticeable it becomes.

A person can be involved in many different types of groups. Sometimes these groups are encouraging, but sometimes they push us toward things we know we shouldn't do. Today we're going to look at which groups and which people we should listen to.

Option 2: Donut Taste Test. For this option, you need several stale and several fresh donuts (make sure you know which ones are stale, but no one else can tell), a knife, a plate and an adult volunteer to supervise.

Ahead of time, cut the donuts into bite-sized pieces and arrange them on the plate. In addition, call five students from your group and let them know you'll be choosing them as volunteers during this step. Their job is to pretend that the stale donuts are the best-tasting ones.

Greet students and ask, "Who likes donuts?" As you're blinded by a sea of raised hands, select eight volunteers (the five you called and three more). Pretend to randomly choose the three new volunteers to go out of the room with the adult volunteer. Explain to the rest of the group that the five remaining volunteers were preselected and that you're going to show students the power of group pressure.

Call one of the three volunteers back into the room and let him or her know that you're going to conduct a donut taste test. Invite all six of the volunteers in the room to taste the two types of donuts, making sure to allow the five preselected ones to go first. (The new one will be pressured to go along with the other five.) Allow for his or her vote; then explain the truth about the test and ask him or her to play along as you call another volunteer in. Repeat the process for the seventh and eighth taste testers; then interview the three volunteers who had to undergo the pressure:

- How did it feel to have everyone else saying that the stale donuts tasted better when you totally disagreed?
- Did the pressure change your answer at all?
- Were you tempted to give in?

Discuss with the entire group whether it is harder to resist peer pressure that's coming from one person or pressure that's coming from a group of people. Explain that group peer pressure is typically harder to resist. Groups of people have a lot of power—in fact, they have so much power that we've got to make sure we know which ones to listen to.

MESSAGE

Option 1: **Wise Advice.** For this option, you need several Bibles, two adult volunteers, a bag of potato chips, two blindfolds and a prize for the winning team (small bags of chips, maybe?).

Divide students into two teams and ask for one volunteer from each team. Inform the volunteers that their task is to cross the room without stepping on any of the chips you will spread across the floor. Ah, that's too easy. Let's blindfold them! They must lift their feet with each step—no shuffling across to move chips out of the way.

Teammates call out instructions to guide their team rep across the room while calling out false instructions to sabotage the other team rep. No one except the two team reps is allowed to step inside the area where the chips are at any time. Blindfold the team reps and then spread several chips on the floor in their pathways. Give the signal to begin and ask the adult volunteers to help you keep track of the number of times the reps step on chips; then declare a winner after they both make it across.

Award the prize to the winning team; then ask the two who crossed how hard it was to discern which voices to listen to. Allow for responses and distribute Bibles. Set the stage by explaining that after King David died, his son Solomon became king. After Solomon died, his son Rehoboam became king of Israel. Ask five volunteers to read through 1 Kings 12:1-20, each reading four verses. Then explain that Rehoboam's problem here was similar to the game: He couldn't figure out which voices to listen to. His father, Solomon, had taxed the people heavily and required his followers to serve as laborers and military soldiers (see 1 Kings 12:4). Discuss the following:

- What kind of advice did Rehoboam get from the elders? *To be a servant to his people.*
- Why do you think he rejected their advice? *He probably viewed servant-hood as weakness and wanted to be absolutely powerful.*
- Who did he turn to? *His peers—people who were about his age.*
- What was their counsel? *To put an even heavier burden on the people.*

Read 1 Kings 11:9-13, and then discuss what word of the Lord was being fulfilled in 1 Kings 12:15. (*The prophecy that the house of David would be punished for Solomon's idolatry and breach of the covenant.*) Ask, "What happened to Rehoboam?" (*He was forced to flee and he lost most of the kingdom to Jeroboam.*)

Explain that it's true that older people who have more life experience tend to give better advice than younger people. This is especially true for older Christians who've had more time to grow in their relationship with the Lord. Christians who are more mature, both in age and in spiritual maturity, are usually good people to rely on for sound advice. If we pay attention to people who are wise, we're bound to make better choices. If not, we'll end up destroyed or wind up hurting people around us—just like Rehoboam.

Option 2: Advice from the Man on the Street. You'll need a TV and a video camera, and whatever other hardware you need (cables, DVD player, computer) to edit and play your man-on-the-street masterpiece. Low-tech option: Use an audio recorder/player instead of video.

Ahead of time, videotape or audiotape children's answers to the following question: "What do you need to remember when you're driving a car?"

Youth Leader Tip

In today's world, peers become influential by default. Today's junior-highers are more influenced by peers and media than ever before because those are the influences most consistent in their lives.

Also videotape or audiotape adults' answers to the same question.

Set the stage by explaining that after King David died, his son Solomon became king. After Solomon died, his son Rehoboam became king of Israel. Then tell the story of King Rehoboam found in 1 Kings 12. Explain that Rehoboam made a bad decision because he listened to the wrong people. We learn a few things about the kind of people we should be listening to from Rehoboam's story.

First, we discover that it is important to listen to those who tell us the truth, not just those who say what we want to hear. Ask, "When we need advice, where do we typically go?" (*We usually go to our friends—and this can be a big mistake.*) While our friends can be a support to us when we have to make tough decisions, they often can't see the situation from all sides. They end up giving advice based more on what they think we want to hear than on what's right.

Illustrate by asking students to pair up and stand back to back. Instruct them to listen for your signal and change one thing about their appearance (e.g., glasses on upside down, shirt buttoned wrong, belt off). When you give the signal again, partners will turn to face each other and the partner who recognizes what's different on his or her partner first will move to the right side of the room; the other partner will sit out. Instruct students still in the game to pair off again and repeat the process of elimination until you have a winner.

Explain that when something is out of place, or wrong with how you look, don't you want to know? When you have that piece of spinach stuck in your teeth or that hair sticking straight up, you want your friends to tell you the truth, right? Of course! King Rehoboam's friends decided not to tell him the truth. They flattered him by telling him that his little finger was thicker than his father's waist—a fancy way of saying that he was more important than his father, King Solomon. Were they telling him the truth? No. Isn't it interesting that most people know about King Solomon, but very few know about his son Rehoboam? Instead of going to people who will tell us what we want to hear, we should go to people who will tell us the truth and give us good advice.

A second thing we learn from Rehoboam's story is that we should listen to those who are experienced, not those who think they know the right answer. Play the video (or audio) interviews and comment on the main difference in the advice people gave: The children (who had no experience) couldn't give real advice about driving but the adults (who were experienced) knew what they were talking about.

Transition to the next step by explaining that Rehoboam heard from two groups, but he decided to listen to those who had less experience. We've probably all received advice from people who had no clue what we were going through or those who had never been in our situation. People often think they have good ideas on what to do, but unless they've been in the situation they're advising on, they really have no idea if their advice will work! The truth is that it's the people who've faced many difficult situations in their lives who can give the best advice.

DIG

Option 1: *Star Wars*. You'll need a TV, a DVD player and a copy of the classic movie *Star Wars.* Ahead of time, cue the video approximately one hour, 51 minutes from the beginning to the scene in which Luke Skywalker blows up the Death Star.

Play the video clip through the scene where Obi-Wan says, "The Force will always be with you" and then discuss the following questions:

- Why did Luke put down the targeting scanner? *Luke heard (or remembered) Obi-Wan telling him to use the Force instead.*
- How do you think Luke would have handled the situation if he hadn't been trained by Obi-Wan? *He probably wouldn't have known what to do.*
- In the Star Wars universe, what does someone have to do to become a Jedi knight? *Go through extensive training with another older and wiser Jedi.*
- When you face peer pressure, do you think about what your parents or other adults have taught you? Why or why not?
- What percent of the time do you actually decide to do what you've been taught?
- Name one situation where you should be living out what wise people have taught you instead of listening to the people who are pressuring you.

Transition by explaining that we all need to remember what wiser, more experienced people have taught us, but we also need to be part of groups that encourage us and help us resist peer pressure. As we close, we're going to look at how the group we're in right now can be that kind of group.

Option 2: Dear Dr. Advice. For this option, you need Copies of "Dear Dr. Advice" (found on the next page), paper and pens or pencils. Ahead of time, cut

Dear Dr. Advice

Dear Dr. Advice,

People at school talk a lot about sex. They say that everybody is doing it—and that people who haven't done it yet are just babies. My youth pastor says it's not true that everybody is doing it and that even a lot of the people talking about it haven't done it. I'm not sure who I should believe. I don't want my friends to think I'm weird. Who should I listen to?

Dear Dr. Advice,

My mom and dad are going away for the weekend and my brother and I get to stay home alone. They say we can't have anyone over while they're gone, but what do they expect me to do—sit home alone the whole weekend? My friends said we should have a small party with just a few people over. What could it hurt to have just a couple of friends over? Aren't my parents being way overprotective and controlling?

Dear Dr. Advice,

Since school started again, I've been getting involved in a lot of partying. Most of the parties I go to have older kids who drink. I know it's against the law—and definitely against what my parents say—but everyone is doing it. I'm always hearing how alcohol would help me to relax and have even more fun. I'm not stupid enough to get in a car with someone who's been drinking, but why can't I have a little at a party?

Dear Dr. Advice,

I'm 12 and I started middle school this year. I've made new friends and they make fun of my best friend from elementary school. We don't hang out much now that we're in middle school, but I don't tease him like my new friends. But I don't defend him, either. I like my new friends and I like my old friend. What should I do?

the handout into individual letters.

Divide students into small groups of three to five and distribute one advice letter, paper and a pen or pencil to each group. Explain that students are writers for an advice chat-room for teens called "Dear Dr. Advice." Groups should discuss possible responses to the letters they received.

Allow a few minutes for brainstorming, and then ask each group to share its letter and advice with the whole group. Discuss the advice given; then explain that, as part of a responsible group of caring friends, we need to give each other good, solid advice that encourages one another to make good decisions and resist negative peer pressure.

APPLY

Option 1: Accountability Groups. For this option, you need volunteers to share testimonies, room enough for each group of six to eight students to meet without overhearing other groups, and one copy of "Accountability Group Questions" (found on the next page) and an adult to act as facilitator for each group.

Ahead of time, arrange for volunteers to share their experiences facing peer pressure. Ideally, the testimonies should include having to make a hard decision in the midst of negative peer pressure and how positive peer encouragement helped in the midst of a tough situation.

Ask the volunteers to share their testimonies and be sure to highlight the difference between trying to stand under pressure alone versus handling it with a friend. Explain that one of the goals of this session is to establish accountability groups. Accountability is just a big word for helping someone really live as a follower of Jesus. In order for accountability groups to work, you must trust one another. Even more important, you must be trustworthy. In order to ensure this, the accountability groups will have two rules:

1. *Total Confidentiality.* Everything said within the group stays within the group—anything said should never be shared with anyone outside of that group, not even with a member of another group.

2. *Total Forgiveness.* When a member of an accountability group confesses to having done something wrong, other members in the group must be committed to completely forgiving that person and encouraging him or her to resist the temptation in the future. No one in an accountability group should ever be judgmental toward

Accountability Group Questions

Select five or six questions to discuss. Remember to keep everyone's answers confidential—don't share them with anyone outside your group.

- Have you spent time praying this week on a regular basis?

- How have you served other people this week?

- Do you treat your peers as people who are loved by God?

- What significant thing did you do for your family this week?

- What was your biggest disappointment this week? How did you decide to handle it?

- What was your biggest joy this week? Did you thank God?

- What do you see as your number one need for next week?

- Did you take time to show compassion for others in need this week?

- Did you control your tongue this week?

- Did you read God's Word this week?

- How have you been tempted this week? How did you respond?

- How has your relationship with Christ been changing during the last week—for good or bad?

- Did you worship in church this week?

- Have you shared your faith this week? How?

- What are you wrestling with in your thought life?

- What have you done for someone else this week?

- Are the visible you and the real you the same person?

- Have you lied in your answers to any of these questions?

another member.

Divide students into small accountability groups and assign each group an adult (or responsible high-school age) facilitator. Distribute "Accountability Group Questions" and send each group to a different area for privacy. Have students select some of the questions on the handout to discuss within their group. *Note:* It's important that the facilitator be a participant and answer the questions just like everyone else.

Allow several minutes for group discussion, then bring everyone back together as a whole group (have the small groups stay close together, though) and establish a time that each group will meet once a week for the next month. A good time might be just before or just after your regular large-group meeting. Have facilitators close the session by leading their accountability groups in prayer.

Note: After a month, meet with the facilitators to evaluate if the groups are meeting their purpose. If so, continue meeting; if not, have them work with you to modify or disband groups that aren't working out.

Option 2: Keep Him Out! For this option, you need patience!

Ask for a volunteer who's pretty physical—but not violent—to come up and stand by you. Instruct the group to form a tight circle in another part of the room. When you give the signal, the volunteer should do everything he can to get inside the circle (give no instructions to the rest of the group). Give the signal and watch as students forming the circle do all they can to keep him out. Call a halt to the madness, and then discuss the following:

- Why was this person kept out of the circle? *"Because you told us to!"* *should be the reply.*
- Did I specifically tell anyone not to let him into the circle? *Well, no, not exactly.*

Explain that the only instructions you gave were to the volunteer. He was to try to penetrate the circle, but you didn't say anything about keeping him out! Continue by pointing out that many groups of friends are this way; somebody wants to become part of the group, but the group does all it can to exclude that person. Positive groups are open to new friends and encourage godly behavior. If you really want to bring your friends to Christ, you must constantly make sure that your group is friendly and inviting for new people to join.

This may be a good time to have a frank discussion about how open the group is to new people. Ask students to think about how often they invite their non-Christian friends, and how comfortable they think their friends would be when visiting the group.

Close by having students form a circle and hold hands. Let go of the hand of the student to one side of you and explain that in breaking the circle this way, the group is symbolizing the openness of the group to new people. Have several students pray for their non-Christian friends. Close with a prayer of covenant for the group to always be open and inviting to newcomers.

Youth Leader Tip

Youth ministries can provide positive relationships and affirmation in the lives of students to help them battle negative peer pressure influence. Because the people they spend time with will have a profound impact on them, they need to choose their friends wisely.[1]

REFLECT

The following short devotions are for the students to reflect on and answer during the week. You can make a copy of these pages and distribute to your class or print out from the PDF available online at **www.gospellight.com/un common/uncommon_jh_friends_and_peer_pressure.zip.**

1—CHOOSE YOUR PATH

Jog over to Proverbs 4:14-15.

Here we are, walking again! What does it mean to "set foot on the path of the wicked or walk in the way of evil men"? What does God want us to do instead of walking with them or being like them?

- ☐ Hightail it out of there.
- ☐ Fall down and play dead.
- ☐ Stop, drop and roll.
- ☐ Shake, rattle and roll.

Think of your friends. You probably wouldn't call them *evil* exactly, but maybe you have a few friends who do stuff that isn't so great. When you hang out with them, you end up doing that wrong stuff, too. Pray for your friends and also ask God to show you how to go His way and to give you the strength to do it! And, just maybe, your friends will follow you on the right path!

2—ONE BAD APPLE

Check out Proverbs 13:20 and 1 Corinthians 15:33.

Have you ever heard the saying "One bad apple spoils the whole bunch"? Well, the Bible says something very similar in the verses you just read.

What do these verses mean? Imagine that you are explaining these verses to an alien from Jupiter. How would you restate these verses so that your new friend from Jupiter could understand them?

_____

_____

_____

_____

Think about the people you hang out with. Are they good or bad influences on you?

_____

_____

_____

_____

_____

Who do you know who helps you stay on track with God in the way you talk, think and act? What about you—how do you influence your friends?

_____

_____

_____

_____

_____

Spend some time praying that God will show you how to be a good influence in your circle of friends today or even that He will give you the strength to find new friends if all of yours constantly pull you down.

3—GIVE COURAGE

Breeze over to Hebrews 3:12-14.

We all need encouragement, right? But what does that word mean anyway? It means "to give courage to." There are lots of things we need courage to do. For instance, you may need courage to speak to that cute girl or guy. Or you might need courage to try out for that sports team or that part in the play. Even more than those things, though, it takes courage to live your life for Jesus.

In the past week or two, has someone given you courage to follow Jesus? Who gave you that encouragement? What was it?

_____

_____

_____

_____

_____

_____

Write your encourager a thank-you note! Also, write down four ways that you can give courage to a friend to live for Jesus, and make sure you do it this week!

_____

_____

_____

_____

_____

_____

4—SPUR EACH OTHER ON

Blow over to Hebrews 10:23-25.
A little poem for you:

Spunky the racehorse had lost her spunk
(It seems she had fallen into some sort of a funk).
So Amber the rider
Sat down astride her
And stuck her spurs in Spunky's rump.

When we spur each other on, we are helping each other to continue living in a way that will please God. God wants us to know that it is so important to have friends to get together with for the purpose of encouraging and spurring each other on!

Who are your two closest Christian friends? What can you do in the next three days to help them please God?

_____

_____

_____

_____

_____

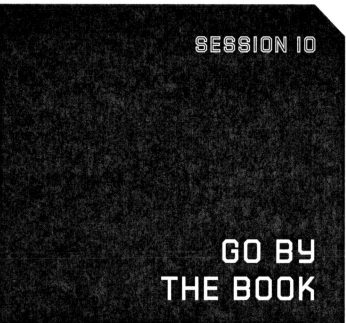

GO BY THE BOOK

THE BIG IDEA
Knowing and applying Scripture can help us resist negative peer pressure.

SESSION AIMS
In this session you will guide students to (1) understand how knowing the Bible can help them resist peer pressure; (2) feel convicted to memorize Scripture to help in tempting situations; and (3) commit to applying Scripture to different temptations they face this week.

THE BIGGEST VERSE
"Jesus answered, 'It is written: "Man does not live on bread alone, but on every word that comes from the mouth of God"'" (Matthew 4:4).

OTHER IMPORTANT VERSES
Deuteronomy 11:18; Psalm 119:9-11; Matthew 4:1-11; Luke 4:1-13; Colossians 3:16; 1 Timothy 6:10; 2 Timothy 3:16; Hebrews 4:12; James 1:22

Note: Additional options and worksheets in 8¹/₂" x 11" format for this session are available for download at **www.gospellight.com/uncommon/jh_friends_and_peer_pressure.zip**.

STARTER

Option 1: Tricky Bible Quiz. For this option, you need paper, pens or pencils, and candy prizes. Greet students and explain that you are going to give them a quick Bible quiz, and anyone who gets the questions all right will win a prize. Instruct students to number their papers from one to six and then ask the following questions (don't give the answers!):

1. Is the book of Hezekiah before or after the book of Psalms?
   Neither, there is no book of Hezekiah in the Bible.

2. Who in the Bible said, "Do unto others as they do unto you"?
   (A) Moses
   (B) Jesus
   (C) Paul
   No one. Jesus said, "Do to others what you would have them do to you" (Matthew 7:12, emphasis added).

3. In what book of the Bible does it say, "Money is the root of all evil"?
   (A) Deuteronomy
   (B) Matthew
   (C) 1 Timothy
   No book. The Bible says, "The love of money is a root of all kinds of evil" (1 Timothy 6:10, emphasis added). If someone gets picky and says that it technically does say "money is a root of all evil" within that phrase, give them credit for a right answer.

4. Which of the Ten Commandments says, "Love your neighbor as yourself"?
   (A) Second
   (B) Fifth
   (C) Eighth
   None of the Ten Commandments. Jesus said this in Luke 10:27, quoting from Leviticus 19:18, which is not part of the Ten Commandments.

5. In what book of the Bible does it say, "God helps those who help themselves"?
   (A) Proverbs
   (B) Ecclesiastes
   (C) 1 Corinthians
   None. That quote is attributed to Ben Franklin.

6. What did Jesus turn stones into?
   (A) Bread
   (B) Fish
   (C) Water
   Jesus never turned stones into anything. He was tempted by Satan to turn them into bread, but He didn't.

Share the correct answers and award a prize if anyone got them all right. If no one did, feel free to award prizes to the student(s) who got the most correct. (That is, unless you want to keep the candy for yourself. Hey, we don't get many perks in youth ministry, so we have to take them where we can find them.) Then discuss the following:

- Do most people in your school know much about the Bible?
- On a scale of 1 to 10, how would you rate your knowledge of the Bible?
- On a scale of 1 to 10, how would you rate what you want your knowledge of the Bible to be? What kinds of things would you have to do to know more?
- How would being more familiar with the Bible affect the way you respond to temptations?

Explain that knowing the Bible well is the first step but, as you'll see today, if we want to stand against peer pressure, we have to apply it as well!

Option 2: Who Wants to Be a Bible-aire? For this option, you need the "Who Wants to Be a Bible-aire?" questions (found on the next page), coins and a few dollar bills to award as prizes. Ahead of time, you might want to make the questions into PowerPoint or Keynote slides so that everyone (including the contestant) can see them.

Greet students and explain that this game is modeled after *Who Wants to Be a Millionaire?* Start with a fastest-time round where several students compete to become the contestant. Whoever raises his or her hand first and then answers correctly gets to be the contestant.

Contestants will have three lifelines. They can (1) poll the audience (where you read each answer and have the audience either raise their hands or cheer for the answer they think is right); (2) 50/50 (where you remove two of the wrong answers) or (3) ask a friend (where the contestant has 60 seconds to ask a friend what he or she thinks is the right answer).

WHO WANTS TO BE A BIBLE-AIRE?

FAST ROUND QUESTIONS

1. **Put these people in the order in which they appear in the Bible:**
   a) Abraham; b) Jacob; c) Isaac; d) Joseph   (Answer: a, c, b, d)
2. **Put these books of the Bible in order:**
   a) Exodus; b) Leviticus; c) Genesis; d) Numbers (Answer: c, a, b, d)
3. **Put these books of the Bible in order:**
   a) Romans; b) John; c) Acts; d) 1 Corinthians   (Answer: b, c, a, d)

CONTESTANT QUESTIONS

1. **What holiday celebrates Jesus' rising from the dead, so we who believe can do the same?**

   a) Christmas; b) Valentine's Day; c) Thanksgiving; d) Easter

2. **How did Judas identify Jesus for the priests?**

   a) Put his arm around him; b) Kissed him; c) Gave him his staff; d) Shook his hand

3. **What is 1 Corinthians 13 all about?**

   a) Love; b) Sin; c) Peace; d) Satan

4. **What did Jesus do in the Garden of Gethsemane?**

   a) Worship; b) Pray; c) Hide; d) Sleep

5. **What teenager was thrown into a pit by his brothers?**

   a) Jacob; b) David; c) Joseph; d) Elijah

6. **"He leads me in the paths of righteousness for his name's _____."**

   a) Holiness; b) Sake; c) Jesus; d) Understanding

7. **Where does the Bible say the final world war will take place?**

   a) Jericho; b) Jerusalem; c) Babylon; d) Armageddon

8. **Which biblical character lived the longest on earth?**

   a) Noah; b) Methuselah; c) Abraham; d) Moses

9. **What was the first plague on Egypt?**

   a) Locusts/grasshoppers: b) Killing of all firstborn; c) Day turned to night; d) River turned to blood

10. **Which of the disciples was a tax collector?**

    a) Mark; b) Matthew; c) Luke; d) John

11. **Which is not a part of the Trinity?**

    a) Father; b) Jesus; c) Holy Ghost; d) Angel

12. **What was the job of Joseph, Mary's husband?**

    a) Carpenter; b) Doctor: c) Innkeeper; d) Janitor

13. **If Eve ate the forbidden fruit, the serpent said she would be like whom?**

    a) Adam; b) God; c) An angel; d) The serpent

14. **Blessed are they that mourn for they shall be _____ .**

    a) Comforted; b) Saved; c) Rich; d) Wise

15. **What father almost sacrificed his own son on an altar?**

    a) Abraham; b) Isaac; c) Lot; d) Aaron

16. **I have hidden your word in my _____ that I might not sin against you.**

    a) Mind; b) Bible; c) Heart; d) Life

17. **What did Jonah tell the sailors would happen if they threw him overboard?**

    a) He would drown; b) He would walk on water; c) God would punish them; d) The sea would be calm.

18. **Which book of the Bible has the most chapters?**

    a) Genesis; b) Psalms; c) Proverbs; d) Revelation

19. **What was the job of Paul?**

    a) Tentmaker; b) Carpenter; c) Accountant; d) Tax collector

20. **Who brought the Ark of the Covenant into Jerusalem?**

    a) Moses; b) Solomon; c) David; d) Indiana Jones

ANSWERS

(1) d; (2) b; (3) a; (4) b; (5) c; (6) b; (7) d; (8) b;
(9) d; (10) b; (11) d; (12) a; (13) b; (14) a; (15) a
(16) c; (17) d; (18) b; (19) a; (20) b.

Here are the money values for each round: first round, 1 cent (make a big deal about this); second round, 2 cents; third round, 3 cents; fourth round, 6 cents; fifth round, 10 cents; sixth round, 15 cents; seventh round, 25 cents; eighth round, 50 cents; ninth round, 75 cents; tenth round, $1.00.

Play all 10 rounds and then transition to the rest of the lesson by explaining that most people today don't know very much about the Bible. In fact, it's been said that half of all Americans cannot name Genesis as the first book of the Bible, and 14 percent think Joan of Arc was Noah's wife. It's too bad that people don't know more about the Bible, because many great people have found it to be an incredible thing to base their lives on. But it's not enough to just know about the Bible; we have to go deeper to really help us know what to do when we face tough questions or temptations.

MESSAGE

Option 1: Repeat After Me. For this option, you need your Bible and a quick mind. Have students stand and try to repeat everything that you say, exactly as you say it—even though it is very strange. If possible, have volunteers monitor whether students say everything properly or not. Anyone who misses must sit down. Start with the first item, and then add one more each time (so the first time you will say, "One hen," the second time, "One hen, two ducks," and so on).

1. One hen
2. Two ducks
3. Three squawking geese
4. Four limerick oysters
5. Five porpulent porpoises
6. Six pairs of Dynal Virgil's tweezers
7. Seven thousand Macedonians in full battle array
8. Eight solid brass monkeys from the sacred, ancient crypts of Egypt
9. Nine sympathetic, apathetic, diabetic old men on roller skates with a marked propensity toward procrastination and sloth
10. Ten lyrical, spherical, diabolical denizens of the deep who stall around the corner of the quo on the quay of the quivy

Award a prize to the student(s) who gets the farthest. Share the importance of being able to memorize vital information (phone numbers, locker combinations, a speech for class, music). Then explain that we all have to memorize things. Usually, we memorize things because it's necessary to have them right when we need them.

Read Matthew 4:4-11. Follow up the story by explaining that the devil makes temptations attractive, just as he did in the first temptation by asking Jesus to turn stones into bread when Jesus was extremely hungry after His 40-day fast.[1] In the second temptation, the devil offered the world to Jesus through an easy path rather than through God's plan. In the third temptation, Satan tempted Jesus to test God's faithfulness and attract attention to Himself. In all three cases, Jesus had memorized Bible verses (see Deuteronomy 8:3; 6:13,16), so He had them when He needed them. Jesus was able to face every temptation the devil threw at Him because He had important verses memorized.

Option 2: Good Memories. For this option, you need a whiteboard, a dry-erase marker and a picture of something that brings a good memory for you (such as a vacation, wedding or birthday). Also, if possible, ask students the week before to bring a picture of a good time in their lives. (It's a good idea to call them during the week to remind them.)

Display the photo and explain what's happening in the picture and why it's a good memory for you. If students have brought pictures, have them share why their pictures are good memories for them. Discuss the following questions:

- Share your earliest memory.
- Tell about a time when you had to memorize something and how you felt about it.
- Memorizing things is easy/hard for me because . . .
- What can you do to help you remember something more easily?
- Is memorizing Bible verses important, or is it enough to just have a pretty close idea of what a Bible verse says?

After the discussion, have someone read the story of Jesus' temptation in Matthew 4:1-11. Follow up the story by explaining that the devil makes temptations attractive, just as he did in the first temptation by asking Jesus to turn stones into bread when Jesus was extremely hungry after His 40-day fast. In the second temptation, the devil offered the world to Jesus through an easy path rather than through God's plan. In the third temptation, Satan tempted Jesus to test God's faithfulness and attract attention to Himself. Discuss the following:

- How did Jesus face Satan's temptations? *He quoted Bible verses.*
- Can you think of a Bible verse that could help you stand up against a temptation? *"Flee sexual immorality," "Don't get drunk with wine," "Do not steal," to name just a few. (Write suggestions on the whiteboard as a visual reminder.)*

DIG

Option 1: Lost in Translation. For this option, you need copies of "Lost in Translation" (found on the next page).

Note: As you probably know from experience, junior-high students love chaos. Instead of passing out papers the way teachers do in school, just take the papers and throw them in the air to various parts of the room. Your students will generally make sure that each person gets one.

If you have had any experience trying to communicate with someone who doesn't speak English well, share a brief story about it. It doesn't have to be funny or profound; it's just important that it's your story. Then explain that sometimes it's hard to translate things between different languages. Things sometimes get lost in the translation. Distribute "Lost in Translation" and have volunteers read some of the mistranslations aloud to the group. Then discuss the following:

- What causes these translations to come out so badly? *Words from one language don't mean exactly the same thing as words in another language; different people interpret words differently; the people who translated these things probably didn't know English very well.*
- How many languages was the Bible written in originally? *Three: Hebrew, Greek and Aramaic.*
- How can we know that it was translated properly? *The English translations were made by large teams of scholars who were fluent in the three languages; any mistranslation would probably be caught by one of the other translators; many believe the Holy Spirit not only inspired the writers of the Bible, but also guided the translators.*
- How does all of this make you feel about the Bible and its accuracy?
- If you believe that the Bible is trustworthy, what difference would that make in the way you use it to stand against peer pressure? *If we know something is true, that makes it a lot easier to consistently obey what it tells us to do and be like.*

LOST IN TRANSLATION

- The name Coca-Cola in China was first rendered as *ke-kou-ke-la.* Unfortunately, the Coke company did not discover until after thousands of signs had been printed that the phrase means "bite the wax tadpole" or "female horse stuffed with wax," depending on the dialect. Coke then researched 40,000 Chinese characters and found a close phonetic equivalent, *ko-kou-ko-le,* which can be loosely translated as "happiness in the mouth."

- A Dutch company attempted to introduce a chocolate bar into the United States called "Zit." It did rather poorly and was quickly withdrawn.

- When General Motors introduced the Nova into the Latin American market, it didn't do well despite the company's extensive brand research. As it turned out, in Spanish "no va" means "it doesn't go."

- An American T-shirt maker in Miami printed shirts for the Spanish market which promoted the Pope's visit. Instead of the desired "I Saw the Pope" in Spanish, the shirts proclaimed "I Saw the Potato."

- When translated into Chinese, the Kentucky Fried Chicken slogan "finger-lickin' good" came out as "eat your fingers off."

- A detour sign in Japan reads: "Stop. Drive sideways."

- A sign in a Copenhagen airline ticket office says: "We take your bags and send them in all directions."

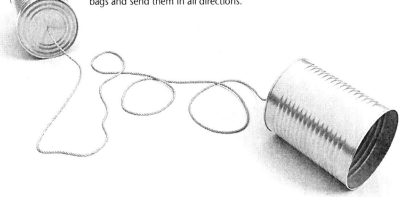

Option 2: True Questions. For this option, you need just these here questions. *Note:* A good resource for difficult questions is Josh McDowell, *The New Evidence That Demands a Verdict* (Nashville, TN: Thomas Nelson, 1999).

1. How can we know the Bible is true? *(1) Because Jesus Christ, God's own Son and our Savior, had complete faith and confidence in the trustworthiness of God's Word (see Matthew 5:17-19). (2) We can know God's Word is true by putting it into practice and experiencing His promises. (3) We can examine the internal consistency of the Bible's message and the external consistency of history and archaeology. (4) We can look at the impact Jesus and the Bible have had on the world throughout history.*

2. How can we know the Bible is the same today as it was when it was first written? *As an ancient document, the Bible is better preserved than any other historical document. There are thousands and thousands of handwritten manuscripts of the Bible that still exist, while there are only very few copies of other ancient documents still around. Also, archaeological findings have confirmed many details of the stories of the Bible. In comparing ancient copies with today's copies there are only minimal differences between the old and the new versions. And yet these external proofs might be disputed by disbelievers, so once again we must trust in the reliability of God's Word as we put it into practice in our own lives and see the results in the lives of others.*

3. Doesn't the Bible contradict itself? *If you look at the Bible as a whole you will see that there is one central theme to the entire Book: God's desire to bring redemption and salvation to humanity. This unifying message is gradually unfolded throughout Scripture until the life, death and resurrection of Jesus Christ brings it all together. When we allow the Bible as a whole speak for itself, these so-called contradictions evaporate.*

4. If the Bible was written in other languages, how can we know that our translation is really what God meant to say? *The English translations were made by large teams of scholars who were fluent in all the languages and these teams cross-checked one another's work to ensure accuracy. A lot of research and study goes into the translation of the*

Bible into any language, often taking many years to accomplish. The Holy Spirit, who inspired the writers of the Bible, also guides the translators today.

5. Given how old the Bible is, how can it still be relevant to the peer pressures we face today? *Great question, but the answer is wrapped up in God Himself. God's been around for a long time—actually, forever—He's just as relevant to us as He was to the very first humans. He doesn't change, and neither does the truth of His Word. When we understand its stories and principles, we can apply them to life in the 5th century, the 12th century or the 21st century.*

APPLY

Option 1: Love Note. For this option, you need several Bibles, a whiteboard, a dry-erase marker, paper and pens or pencils. Ahead of time, write the following list on the whiteboard:

- Focusing on physical appearance: 1 Samuel 16:7; 1 Timothy 2:9-10; 1 Peter 3:1-7
- Cheating: Leviticus 6:1-5; 19:36; Proverbs 11:1; 1 Corinthians 6:7-8
- Drinking/drugs: Proverbs 23:29-35; 31:4-7; Ephesians 5:18; 1 Peter 4:3-4
- Gossip: Exodus 23:1; Proverbs 25:18; 2 Thessalonians 3:11-12; Titus 3:1-2

Share the following story:

Imagine you're just hanging out with friends, when all of a sudden the most beautiful girl (or the most handsome guy) in school walks right up to you. He or she says, "Hi. I've had my eye on you for a while, and I think you're cute. I want to get to know you better. I'd like you to come over and have dinner at my house tomorrow night. Here's a map to my house and the address. Come over at 6:00 P.M. Don't be late!"

He or she then hands you a note and walks away, giving you a little wink over the shoulder. You open up the note, and it is the messiest thing you have ever seen! The handwriting is so bad you can't understand a word, much less where the streets are!

Ask, "What would you do? Would you toss the note and skip the dinner date or would you do all you could to find out where the house is?" Allow for responses, and then explain that, as strange as it may sound, many people approach the Bible in just the same way as the people who might just throw the note away. They honestly want to have a relationship with God, but sometimes the Bible just seems too hard to figure out. So they leave it on a shelf, and it does them no good whatsoever. The Bible isn't always easy to figure out, but the result is worth the search.

Divide students into groups of four to six. Distribute Bibles, paper and pens or pencils, and then explain that each of the topics on the board deals with a different peer pressure situation. Have each group choose one of the topics listed to research (more than one group can choose the same topic, but make sure all of the topics are represented) and look up the verses for their topic; then write down in one sentence what the Bible says about it. Have adult volunteers help groups that may have difficulty. After a few minutes, have groups share their results with the whole group.

Guide students in a time of silent prayer, confessing to God a peer pressure situation that they're tempted to give in to and asking God to help them live out what the Bible says.

Option 2: Acting Like an Atheist. For this option, you need paper and pens or pencils. Instruct students to form pairs. Explain as you distribute paper and a pen or pencil to each pair, "On this paper, write out a few sentences describing a really tough peer pressure situation that a Christian junior-higher is likely to face at school."

After a few minutes, have pairs switch papers. Explain that atheists are people who don't believe in God. Unfortunately, sometimes even Christians act like atheists; we act like God isn't around to guide and help us. Take a few minutes to discuss this situation with your partner and write down how an atheist would respond.

After a few minutes, continue by explaining that, hopefully, those in this room will act differently. Why? Because we're trying to obey God's Word. Now take a few minutes to discuss and then write down how someone would act who believed the Bible was true and was committed to letting it affect his or her behavior.

When the pairs are finished, ask a few to share their answers with the rest of the group. Close in prayer, asking God to help us all act like Jesus would want us to when we face tough peer pressure situations this week.

REFLECT

The following short devotions are for the students to reflect on and answer during the week. You can make a copy of these pages and distribute to your class or print out from the PDF available online at **www.gospellight.com/un common/uncommon_jh_friends_and_peer_pressure.zip.**

1—NEED A LIGHT?

Take yourself to Psalm 119:105.

It was a cold night in early September, and Jan sat shivering in the tent. *Oh man,* she thought, *I really have to go to the bathroom!*

Unfortunately, on this hastily planned camping trip, no one had thought to bring a flashlight. Finally, though, Jan could stand it no longer.

"I can't wait for daylight," she said aloud as she got up quickly and stumbled out of the tent.

However, as careful as she was during her daring trip to find the camp bathrooms, she stumbled and tripped, got mixed up in her direction and actually ended up back at the tent, where she finally gave up hope completely—and ended up using a poison oak bush for a restroom, which explains why she is not at school today.

And all because she didn't have a flashlight!

More important than a flashlight on a camping trip is God's Word. When has God's Word shown you the truth and comforted you?

_____

_____

_____

_____

_____

How can you comfort others with what you have learned this week?

_____

_____

_____

_____

_____

2—ON THE WALL

Head into Deuteronomy 11:18-21.

You can tell a lot about a person by what they put on the walls in their room. We surround ourselves with the things that are important to us. What is on the walls of your bedroom or the walls of friends? Pictures of friends and family? Maybe posters of celebrities, sports heroes, music groups or solo artists? Perhaps you have even decorated your room with trophies and ribbons you've won from various events and activities.

God wants us to make His Word important to us, too. Why? Because it guides us in decision making, reminds us of His love for us and teaches us about who He is.

Find a Bible verse that has stuck in your mind and heart from these past few lessons and make a poster out of it for your room. Use lots of color and be creative!!

3—PUT ON YOUR GEAR

Read Ephesians 6:10-18.

In the past, a coat of armor was critical for soldiers in battle—both for the sake of protection (the defense) and for attacking the enemy (the offense). Think of football pads! In the passage you have just read, Paul described Christians as people wearing armor in a battle, with each piece of armor being a different part of the Christian life.

What is the Bible—God's Word—depicted as?

_____

_____

_____

_____

_____

Why do you think Paul chose this piece of a soldier's uniform for the Bible?

_____

_____

_____

_____

If you were Paul writing this letter to the Ephesians, what piece of a soldier's uniform would you have chosen to represent God's Word? Why?

_____

_____

_____

_____

_____

Spend some time today thanking God for His written Word!

4—OPEN WIDE

Spear Hebrews 4:12-13.

"Scalpel please," said Dr. Spurtenbludenguts to her assistant, Nurse John Doughboy. Now, Nurse John Doughboy was new to the surgical ward, so he gave the clamps to Dr. Spurtenbludenguts instead.

"No, no," Dr. Spurtenbludenguts corrected the mistaken Nurse John Doughboy. "I need the scalpel. Let me describe it for you. It is a very sharp, knifelike tool that surgeons use to open a patient up. Without the scalpel, I cannot see what is inside this patient and correct the problem that is ailing him."

"Aaaah," said Nurse John Doughboy, handing her the scalpel.

"Now we'd better hurry up," said Dr. Spurtenbludenguts, "because it looks like our patient is waking up!"

Like the scalpel in this story, God uses His Word to "open us up" and help us see what is wrong inside of us. While this is often painful, it is also very helpful so that we can live full and healthy lives as we seek to follow Him.

Has God ever used His Word to get you back on track? When and how?

_____

_____

_____

_____

This week, ask a friend or an adult you know about a time God used His Word in his or her life to correct him or her and help him or her through a difficult time. Make sure you share your story, too.

PLUG IN TO REAL POWER

THE BIG IDEA

The Holy Spirit gives us strength to resist negative peer pressure.

SESSION AIMS

In this session you will guide students to (1) know how the Holy Spirit can help them when they face peer pressure; (2) feel confident knowing that the Spirit is always with them; and (3) act on what the Holy Spirit tells them to do this week.

THE BIGGEST VERSE

"Then Peter, filled with the Holy Spirit, said to them: 'Rulers and elders of the people!'" Acts 4:8.

OTHER IMPORTANT VERSES

1 Samuel 16:13; 2 Chronicles 16:9; Psalm 118:22; Isaiah 41:10; Matthew 10:17-20; Luke 11:13; John 10:14; 14:16-17; Acts 3:1-10; 4:5-20; 15:32; Romans 8:26; Galatians 5:22-23

Note: Additional options and worksheets in 8$^1/_2$" x 11" format for this session are available for download at **www.gospellight.com/uncommon/jh_friends_and_peer_pressure.zip**.

STARTER

Option 1: Houdini's Secret. For this option, you need an adult volunteer, a pair of sturdy handcuffs (and a key!) and a crisp $10 bill (don't worry; there's only a slim chance that you'll actually lose your money). Ahead of time, let the volunteer know that the secret to getting out of the handcuffs is to say, "Please help."

Note: What?! You don't have a pair of handcuffs? Every self-respecting youth worker should have a pair. Most novelty shops carry them, but make sure you get sturdy ones that really work—you never know when you might need them!

Greet students and show them the handcuffs. Explain that there is a secret to getting out of these handcuffs—whoever can figure out the secret will win $10. Ask for volunteers (check the pulse of anyone not raising his or her hand!). Select a volunteer and place the handcuffs on him or her (tighten them securely, but comfortably). Give the signal and allow 30 seconds for the student to remove the handcuffs. Repeat the process for several students (no one should be able to figure out the secret—this is why you'll need a sturdy pair of handcuffs).

After several students have failed, invite the adult volunteer to come forward and demonstrate the secret; then explain that the secret to getting out of this situation was simply asking for help from the person with the key. Life can be that way, too; sometimes we face difficult situations where people are pressuring us to do something we know is wrong and we feel like we're all alone. The truth is that we're not alone. As you'll see today, God has promised that His Spirit will be with us to help during those hard times when we're pressured and tempted to do the wrong thing.

Option 2: Towel Toss. For this option, you need a towel.

Greet students and have everyone sit in one circle. Explain that you're going to play a game of Towel Toss.[1] Select a student to be It and ask him or her to sit in the middle of the circle. Give the towel to one of the students in the circle and explain that when you give the signal, students forming the circle should toss the towel back and forth to keep It from touching either the towel or the person holding it. If the person in the middle catches the towel or touches someone holding it, the person who threw it or was touched is now It.

Play for a few minutes; then bring another student into the middle of the circle. The new student and It will now work as a team. Begin again and allow several minutes for students to play; then end the game and explain that sometimes life can be similar to this game—we can feel like we're in the middle and that everyone else is doing something against what we're trying to do. Just as someone came in to help the person in the middle during the game, God's Holy Spirit helps us by being there when we face difficult situations. Today you're going to look at how the Holy Spirit even helps us know what to say when we face pressure situations.

MESSAGE

Option 1: Balloon Blizzard. For this option, you need several Bibles, lots of room for students to lie down flat, a balloon for each student (bigger balloons are better), a CD or mp3 of fast music and a CD- or mp3-player. Ahead of time, a few days before the meeting, blow up and tie one balloon so that it will be at least partly deflated for this exercise.

Distribute balloons and instruct students to blow them up and tie them off. Have everyone lie down on his or her back on the floor and explain that they are going to try to keep all the balloons up in the air for as long as they can *without lifting their backs off the floor.* Hands, feet or any other body part can be used and students can even shuffle around the floor on their backs, but they must keep their backs on the floor's surface. Give the signal to begin by starting the music and see how long students can keep all of the balloons in the air.

Let students play a few rounds, and then have students sit on their balloons and pop them all at once. Show the balloon you prepared a few days before and explain that when we face peer pressure, it's kind of like this balloon. It is deflated because the air pressure on the *outside* of the balloon is greater than the air pressure *inside.* Blow up a new balloon and explain that a new balloon stays inflated because the pressure on the inside equals the pressure on the outside. When we face negative peer pressure, we need to rely on the Holy Spirit to give us the internal pressure needed to help us stand firm against what's being pushed on us from the outside.

Youth Leader Tip

Young teens need help in forming their moral convictions. As we help students develop a proper self-image, we will help them be able to choose to say no to the pressures that are permeating our society today.[2]

Distribute Bibles and share the story in Acts 4:5-20 about Peter and John appearing before the Sanhedrin to answer for healing the beggar by the Temple (see Acts 3:1-10). Explain that the Sanhedrin was comprised of rulers, elders and teachers of the Law—a kind of Israel Supreme Court. This put Peter and John—two unschooled and ordinary men (see Acts 4:13)—up against some pretty smart people. Because they were filled with the Holy Spirit, however, what should have been an intimidating situation was easy for them to handle. The Holy Spirit gave them the right words to say when they had to respond. Not only were they able to share the story of Jesus' crucifixion and resurrection, but they were also able to show how Jesus fulfilled Old Testament prophecy, an important element in early Christian sermons and defenses (see Acts 4:8-11). They were so compelled by the Holy Spirit to speak that even when the Sanhedrin commanded them not to share any more about Jesus, they said they could not "help speaking about what we have seen and heard" (Acts 4:20).

Continue by explaining that God can and will give us the right words to say; all we have to do is to listen for Him. Next we're going to discover how we can hear the voice of God through the Holy Spirit . . .

Option 2: *Liar, Liar.* You'll need several Bibles, a TV, a DVD player and a copy of the movie *Liar, Liar.* Ahead of time, cue the video approximately 22 minutes from the beginning to the scene where the main character (played by Jim Carrey) enters the courtroom. The clip you'll be playing will last approximately four minutes.

Note: This video contains sexual references. Review the clip you'll be using for this exercise and edit (fast forward) as appropriate for your group.

Play the clip and then discuss these questions:

• Have you had a time when you couldn't say what you wanted to say?
• Have you had to speak in front of a group of people? What happened?

Explain that the number-one fear of people in America is public speaking. Number two is death. People are more afraid of speaking at funerals than being the dead person at them! Weird, huh? Discuss, "Are you afraid of speaking in front of groups? Why?"

Explain that we have all had times when we can't really express what we want to say. Maybe it's when you were on the phone with that special guy or girl, or maybe it was when people were trying to pressure you into doing something you know you shouldn't. There's a great story in the Bible about two guys who faced some pressure, and knew exactly what to say—because God's Spirit filled them.

Distribute Bibles and ask four volunteers to read through Acts 4:5-20 (each reading four verses). Explain that the Sanhedrin was comprised of rulers, elders and teachers of the Law—a kind of Israel Supreme Court. This put Peter and John—two unschooled and ordinary men (see Acts 4:13)—up against some pretty smart people. Discuss the following:

- What enabled Peter to speak so boldly in Acts 4:8? *The Holy Spirit.*
- How would you summarize what Peter said in verses 8 through 11? *He explained the story of Jesus' crucifixion and resurrection—and how Jesus fulfilled Old Testament prophecy from Psalm 118:22.*
- How would you describe Peter and John? *Ordinary men filled with the extraordinary Holy Spirit (see Acts 4:13).*
- How did Peter and John respond to the Sanhedrin's command to stop speaking about Jesus? *They refused to stop, claiming that they could not "help speaking about what we have seen and heard" (Acts 4:20).*

Isn't it cool that the Holy Spirit can actually give us words to say when we're in difficult situations? Now you're going to find out how we can listen to what the Holy Spirit says to us.

DIG

Option 1: Across a Crowded Room. For this option, you need some loud students (a tall order, we know!).

Have students form a large circle; then assign each student a partner directly across from him or her in the circle. Instruct students to sit down where they are and proceed to find out three pieces of personal trivia from their across-the-room partners: (1) middle name, (2) favorite dessert and (3) favorite band. Explain that partners can communicate however they want, but they are not allowed to move from where they're sitting. Give the signal to begin and allow one minute of information gathering; then give the signal to stop and discuss the following:

- How many of you found out all three things about your partner?
- What techniques did you use to communicate? *Lip reading, sign language, shouting louder than everyone else.*

- What made the communication difficult? *Too much noise in the room, too many conflicting messages.*
- How does this activity relate to our topic of hearing the Holy Spirit? *The Holy Spirit usually communicates as the still, small voice; we often don't allow ourselves to be quiet enough to hear Him.*
- What can we do to better hear the Holy Spirit? *Spend quiet time alone; don't immediately turn on the radio or TV when you walk in a room; pray and ask God to speak to you; then wait and listen.*

Continue by saying, "We're going to end this session by looking at how we can be ready to act when the Holy Spirit speaks to us."

Option 2: Ethan's Trilemma. For this option, you need just this *libro* (that's "book" in Spanish). Share the following case study:

Ethan has gone to church for as long as he can remember, but he does not pray or read his Bible very much. In fact, the only time he *really* prays is when he's in trouble and needs God to bail him out.

Ethan wanted to earn some extra money, so he took a paper route near his home. Most people paid when he went to their house collecting, but Mrs. Sanchez worked evenings, so she always left her money in the mailbox for Ethan to pick up. Even though the paper cost $15 a month, Mrs. Sanchez always left him a $20 bill—she had told Ethan that she would give him an extra $5 every month if he brought the paper right up to the front door instead of leaving it on the curb.

One day, Ethan picked up the envelope in the mailbox as usual, and when he opened it, he noticed there were actually *two* $20 bills stuck together in the envelope. Ethan wasn't sure what to do—had Mrs. Sanchez made a mistake by putting the extra $20 in the envelope?

Ethan asked his friend, Luke, who replied, "Who cares if she meant to put it in there? It's yours now! It's not like she's hurting for money!"

Lauren, Ethan's sister, told him that he should definitely give it back, but he thought maybe she was just jealous because he had the extra money and she didn't.

His mom said, "Why don't you just talk to her and ask her if it was a gift?" But he thought it would be pretty embarrassing to ask her about it.

Ethan was so confused!

Discuss the following: "What do you think God might have told Ethan if he had asked?" (*He should go talk to Mrs. Sanchez so he would know for sure.*) Continue by saying, "Ethan was hearing lots of advice from many sources. How could he have practiced listening for God's voice? (*He could have spent more time walking and talking with God instead of turning to Him only when he was in trouble.*)

Explain that it's important to be close to God so that we can hear the voice of His Spirit when He speaks. Let's take a look at how to be ready to act when He speaks to us . . .

APPLY

Option 1: Seasick. For this option, you need gift Bibles (optional), an adult volunteer (to make the game more difficult, the volunteer should be the same gender as you) and space for junior-highers to run around.

Explain that you're going to end this session with a game called "Seasick." Here's how to play: Students must run to a wall in the room corresponding to a nautical term. Huh? Okay, "bow" is the front; "stern" is the back; "port" is the left side and "starboard" is the right! If, at any time, you call out "Cap'n on deck," students must stand still where they are and salute. The last person to salute is out. Not so hard, right? Wrong. The adult volunteer is also going to be calling out commands. Anyone caught obeying his or her commands instead of yours—the cap'n!—is out.

Play until you have a winner; then explain that this game demonstrates what Jesus meant when He said, "I know my sheep and my sheep know me" (John 10:14). Say, "You've listened to my voice during this whole session; you're familiar with it. If you listened very carefully during the game, you would recognize my voice over any others. It's the same with God; the closer we get to Jesus, the more we hear the voice of His Spirit."

Youth Leader Tip

Nothing turns off unchurched students more than being preached at! While you are called to speak the truth, be very careful to not be judgmental or condemning. Remember, your job is to plant the seeds. God will do the watering through your slow and steady infusion of biblical truths.

You can close the session in prayer, asking the Holy Spirit to speak to each of the students and to make them ready to obey when He speaks, or use this opportunity to invite students who have not yet accepted Jesus into their lives as Lord and Savior to do so now. If you chose to offer an invitation for students to accept Christ, say, "There may be some of you right now who are feeling the Holy Spirit calling you to submit your lives to God. You've tried to live on your own and it hasn't worked out so well. You need a Savior to help you to overcome your sin and have a right relationship with God." Ask everyone to close their eyes and bow their heads in prayer, and then invite those who want to ask Jesus into their lives to raise their hands and silently repeat the following prayer:

Lord Jesus, I know I'm a sinner. I know that I can't possibly have eternal life in heaven without accepting You as my Lord and Savior. Please come into my heart, Jesus, and wash me clean from my sins. Make me new in You and help me to begin a new life right now following Your guidance. Amen.

Invite those who committed their lives to Christ just now to see you after the session. Give them a gift Bible. Be sure to note their names and phone numbers or email addresses so that you can connect with them in the upcoming weeks to encourage their walk in Christ!

Option 2: Juicy Fruit. For this option, you need two pieces of Juicy Fruit gum for each student, copies of "Juicy Fruit—Galatians 5:22-23" (found on the following page) and pens or pencils.

Distribute "Juicy Fruit—Galatians 5:22-23" and pens or pencils. Explain that when we're faced with peer pressure situations, the qualities of the Holy Spirit should show through us. How do we know what they are? Explain that one of the best checklists to see if the Holy Spirit is working through us is found in Galatians 5:22-23.

Allow three minutes for students to complete the handout; then divide the group into small groups of four to six. Members in each group are to share the area that they feel they're doing the best in and the area they most need to work on.

Instruct groups to close in prayer, each member praying for the person on his or her right. After the prayer, distribute two pieces of gum to each student. They can chew one piece now, but challenge them to carry the other piece with them throughout the week to remind them to show the fruit of the Spirit in their lives.

JUICY FRUIT

GALATIANS 5:22-23

How much fruit of the Spirit do you show in your life? Rate each fruit on a scale of 1 (Help! I need a map to the spiritual produce aisle!) to 10 (Gonna have to open up a fruit stand pretty soon!).

LOVE

_____ I willingly sacrifice my own desires in order to serve others.

JOY

_____ I have joy deep inside regardless of the situation on the outside.

PEACE

_____ I feel an inner quiet no matter what situation I find myself in.

PATIENCE

_____ I don't get angry when people try to upset me and I don't entertain thoughts of getting even.

KINDNESS

_____ I help people in need.

GOODNESS

_____ I do the morally right things and obey God's commands.

FAITHFULNESS

_____ I am trustworthy and reliable.

GENTLENESS

_____ I'm not harsh or impatient with people.

SELF-CONTROL

_____ I exercise discipline and resist temptation.

REFLECT

The following short devotions are for the students to reflect on and answer during the week. You can make a copy of these pages and distribute to your class or print out from the PDF available online at **www.gospellight.com/un common/uncommon_jh_friends_and_peer_pressure.zip**.

1—GOOD COUNSELOR

Check out John 14:16-17.

Have you ever gone to camp and had a camp counselor? Maybe you have counselors at your school. Did you know that God has given you His Spirit as a counselor? What is the job of a counselor anyway?

❐ To tell you whatever you want to hear whenever you want to hear it
❐ To tell you the truth, to help you and to comfort you
❐ To be your butler and make your every heart's desire come true

Spend some time thanking God for the gift of His Holy Spirit. Talk to God about some of the situations you are in where you feel peer pressure—and ask Him for His help!

2—CRISIS = OPPORTUNITY

Trot over to 1 Corinthians 2:11-13.

Jessie hangs out at school with a group of friends who like to pull pranks. It has been fun in the past—like the time they hung Sarah's teddy bear collection by their necks in her closet or when they TP'd the youth pastor's house (helping to clean it up the next morning, of course). But this time Jessie doesn't feel so good about their prank. Jessie has a bad feeling in his stomach as they all prepare to go out to the teachers' parking lot and key Mrs. Santiago's car. Heart beating, mind racing, Jessie swallows hard and . . .

What would you do or say at this point?

_____

_____

_____

_____

Sometimes a bad situation can become an opportunity for us to reveal God's truth to our friends. The great thing is that God doesn't put us out there on our own but gives us guidance by His Holy Spirit. That's why Jessie wasn't feeling so good about this prank. If you were in Jessie's position, what you would say to your friends?

_____

_____

_____

_____

3—CHANGE DIRECTION

Cruise to Zechariah 4:6.

Have you ever tried to break a bad habit? Well, Jamie had a problem with cursing. She cursed all the time—she had a total potty mouth! One day, she asked a friend to pull her hair (to really yank a handful!) every time she said a curse word. And she stopped cursing—when her friend was around to pull her hair, that is.

The truth is that when we try to do things in our own strength—like breaking bad habits or standing up to peer pressure—we will fail. If we don't fail right away, we certainly will down the line. We need God's Spirit to work in us and make us strong!

Train yourself to rely on the Holy Spirit today! Think of two situations in which it is hard for you not to follow the crowd. Write down those two situations and today's verse on a small piece of paper and carry it with you to remind you to pray for strength and guidance in those times. When you get into those situations, pray at that moment, too!

4—GOOD CHOICE, BETTER CHOICE

Flip over to Galatians 5:16-17. Every day we make a ton of choices. Write down five choices that you have made so far today, such as what clothes to wear, what to have for breakfast, and so on.

_____

_____

_____

_____

The passage you have just read says that you have yet another choice to make that you may not have even known about. What is it?

_____

_____

_____

_____

_____

_____

It is easy to know which is the better choice in Galatians 5:16-17, but it is not always easy to make the right choice! To encourage you, though, when you choose to live by the Spirit, know that it becomes easier to make that choice every day. Take a few minutes to memorize Galatians 5:16-17.

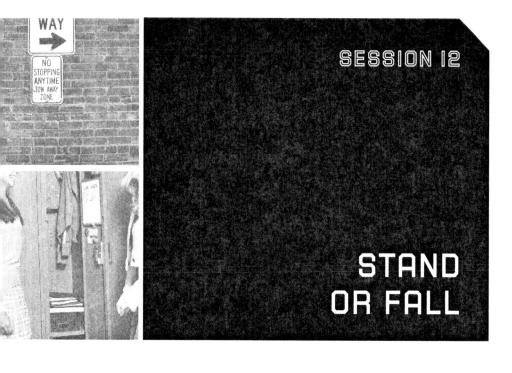

STAND OR FALL

THE BIG IDEA

Knowing who you are in Christ and what you believe helps you resist peer pressure.

SESSION AIMS

In this session you will guide students to (1) examine their beliefs about their own identity in Christ; (2) sense confidence in who they are as followers of Jesus; and (3) feel convicted to act differently this week because of their beliefs.

THE BIGGEST VERSE

"About midnight Paul and Silas were praying and singing hymns to God, and the other prisoners were listening to them" (Acts 16:25).

OTHER IMPORTANT VERSES

Mark 9:24; John 20:27; Acts 9:3-6; 16:16-36; Romans 12:1-2; 2 Timothy 1:12; James 2:23

Note: Additional options and worksheets in 8^1/$_2$" x 11" format for this session are available for download at **www.gospellight.com/uncommon/jh_friends_and_peer_pressure.zip**.

STARTER

Option 1: Who Am I? For this option, you need self-adhesive nametags, a felt-tip pen, a CD or mp3 of lively music and a CD- or mp3-player. Ahead of time, prepare a nametag for each student, using the names of famous people that students will know (e.g., actors, singers, authors, sports stars—don't forget yourself!).

Greet students as they come in and stick a nametag on the back of each student. Explain that each student has to figure out whose name is on the tag on his or her back by asking other students only yes or no questions. (For example, "Am I an actor?") No misleading answers allowed!

Once a student has correctly identified the name on his or her tag, he or she should act like that famous person. Encourage students to ham it up! Start the music and enjoy the confusion!

Allow time for all students to figure out whose famous name is on their backs and to act like that person; then settle everyone down and explain that who we think we are definitely changes how we act. In our everyday lives, sometimes it's hard to really know who we are. We might know our names, what our favorite color is, how tall we are and where we live—but we don't always know what we really believe.

Conclude by stating that today, we're going to see how knowing who we are and what we really believe makes all the difference in how we respond to peer pressure—and how our identity determines our actions.

Option 2: The Eyes Have It. For this option, you need a large sheet of poster board, several copies of magazines featuring celebrities (you can probably get some older ones from your doctor's or dentist's office), scissors, glue, paper, pens or pencils, and candy prizes.

Ahead of time, find pictures of at least 10 famous people and carefully cut out just the eye area of each picture. (Important: Note the name of the person

Youth Leader Tip
Help students understand that once they become Christians, they are children of God, with all the rights and privileges of any of His other children. They are released from being so self-absorbed and can now make a difference in the world. They are free to love as God loves.[1]

the eyes belong to on the back as you go!) Also, number each picture (yes, name and number). Got it? Good. Create an identity key for yourself by noting each picture's number and the corresponding person's identity on a piece of paper. But wait, we're not done yet! Now glue the pictures on the poster board and write only each picture's number below as you go. (Now do you see why you need the identity key?)

Greet students and ask, "How much can you tell about people just by looking at their eyes?" Distribute paper and pens or pencils and point out the poster board. Explain that when you give the signal, students are going to try to guess the famous owner of each pair of eyes. Give the signal to begin and allow a couple of minutes for students to guess as many of the famous names as they can.

Note: You can make this exercise a little easier by providing a list of the famous people for students to choose from.

Allow a couple of minutes; then give the signal for students to stop writing. Call out the correct identity of each pair of eyes and award candy to the student(s) who identified the most. Discuss:

- What does "the eyes are the windows of the soul" mean? *It means that you can sometimes tell a lot about a person's character (honesty, integrity) from his or her eyes.*
- How do you feel when someone looks directly into your eyes for a long time? *Sometimes it can feel as though the person is looking straight through us to our innermost thoughts and feelings.*

Explain that although our eyes can tell a lot about us, our beliefs tell even more. Our beliefs affect our actions—and our actions reveal the most about our character. Today you're going to look at how knowing who you really are determines how you act when faced with peer pressure.

MESSAGE

Option 1: Jailbreak. For this option, you need a Bible, a table, a glass of water, building blocks and 10 action figures (the more outrageous, the better *and* they should have removable pieces of clothing) to represent the following characters: Paul, Silas, a slave girl, the slave girl's owner, a magistrate, two guards, the jailer and the jailer's wife and son.

Ask for several volunteers to help you act out a Bible story about Paul and Silas using the action figures (just for fun, assign two figures per volunteer) and one or two volunteers to build a jail while the action is going on. Read Acts 16:16-36 and have the volunteers use the action figures where indicated. When you reach the part where there's an earthquake, reach over and shake the table violently so that the jail falls apart. Use the glass of water to baptize the jailer's family.

When you're done with the story, emphasize how amazing it was that even after Paul and Silas had been beaten, whipped and thrown in jail, they were able to pray and sing hymns. They didn't wallow in self-pity over what had happened to them. They believed that God loved them and would take care of them no matter what. Explain that even after the miraculous earthquake, Paul and Silas knew it would be wrong to leave the prison, because the jailer would be killed for letting them escape. So they stayed, shared their faith with him, and he and his family became part of God's family.

Paul and Silas knew who they were—followers of Jesus. And their behavior in the jail really demonstrated their belief. Even in the midst of suffering and persecution, they continued to praise God and do what was right. They wouldn't give in to any pressure to relinquish their faith because they were confident in who they were and what they believed.

Challenge students to begin considering their own faith by asking, "Would your convictions stand up to the kind of pressures that Paul and Silas faced?" Continue by stating, "Today we're going to look at how knowing who you really are determines how you act when faced with peer pressure."

Option 2: The Scorpion and the Frog. For this option, you need several Bibles. Read the following Aesop's fable, titled "The Scorpion and the Frog":

A scorpion and a frog meet on the bank of a stream and the scorpion asks the frog to carry him across on its back. The frog asks, "How do I know you won't sting me?" The scorpion replies, "Because if I sting you, I will die too."

The frog, satisfied with the scorpion's answer, agrees to give the scorpion a ride.

When they hit midstream, the scorpion stings the frog. The frog feels the onset of paralysis and starts to sink, knowing they both will drown, but has just enough time to gasp, "Why?"

The scorpion replies, "It's my nature."

At the conclusion of the story, discuss the following:

- What did the scorpion mean when he said, "It's my nature"? *He had to act according to what he was, even if it meant he would die.*
- Was the frog stupid to give the scorpion a ride across the river? Why or why not?
- Do you think the scorpion knew he would end up stinging the frog? *He may have wanted to believe he could refrain from acting on his natural instincts, so he chose to think he had everything under control.*
- Do people always act like who they are? *People don't always act according to what they say they are or what they say they believe, but they almost always act in accordance with what they truly are and what they truly believe. The scorpion professed to be someone who would not sting the frog, but in the end he acted in character with who he truly was.*

Distribute Bibles and ask students to turn to the story of Paul and Silas in Acts 16:16-36. Read through the passage as a group, each student reading one verse. When you're done with the story, emphasize how amazing it was that even after Paul and Silas had been beaten, whipped and thrown in jail, they were able to pray and sing hymns. They didn't wallow in self-pity over what had happened to them. They believed that God loved them and would take care of them no matter what. Explain that even after the miraculous earthquake, Paul and Silas knew it would be wrong to leave the prison, because the jailer would be killed for letting them escape. So they stayed, shared their faith with him, and he and his family became part of God's family.

Paul and Silas were followers of Jesus Christ, and no amount of pressure—not even physical pain—could make them act otherwise. In the midst of all that, they continued to pray, sing hymns and trust God.

Explain that when the pressure is on, who we are determines how we act. We will act according to our true nature when people try to pressure us into doing things that we shouldn't. Conclude by saying, "Will you be like Paul and Silas? They knew who they were in Christ and wouldn't give in to the pressure. Not only do we act according to our nature, but we are also going to look at how the strength of what we believe determines how strongly we can resist negative peer pressure."

DIG

Option 1: *Indiana Jones and the Last Crusade.* You'll need a TV, a DVD player and the movie *Indiana Jones and the Last Crusade.*

Ahead of time, cue the video approximately one hour and 43 minutes from the beginning to the scene where the character Donovan says, "The grail is mine, and you're going to get it for me." This is the six-minute scene where Donovan shoots Professor Jones and Indiana Jones goes through three tests to get the Holy Grail. The third test is the step of faith where Indy must step into open air in order to prove his belief.

Show the clip, and then discuss:

- What did Donovan mean when he said, "It's time to ask yourself what you believe." *If Indy really believed the grail could heal his father, he would go after it.*
- Which would have been the hardest test for you to take?
- Why was Indiana Jones so confident about how to face each challenge? *He followed the instructions in his father's diary and trusted that his father was correct.*

Ask, "Have you ever wondered what your life would be like if you had as much confidence in the instructions given in our Father's book as Indiana Jones had in his father's diary?" Explain that we may *say* that we believe in God and what His Word says, but do we *believe* enough to be able to face the pressures that people put on us? Let's take a look at how you can apply what you believe to specific peer pressure situations . . .

Option 2: Extenuating Circumstances. For this option, you need this book! Share the following case study:

Andrea's best friend, Amber, is usually a pretty good student, but lately she's having some problems getting her homework done because her parents have been fighting so much. Last night Amber didn't study at all for the big math test today. In fact, she spent the whole night crying with her head buried under her pillow, trying not to hear her dad beating on her mom.

As Andrea and Amber enter their first period math class, Amber asks Andrea to let her copy off her test paper just this once. Andrea knows that Amber's a good student and she knows how hard Amber's had it lately, but she's really torn. She wants to help her friend, but she knows cheating is wrong. She finally decides that it's okay to let Amber copy just this once.

Discuss the following:

- Is it *ever* okay to cheat? (Allow for responses.)
- What could Andrea have done differently? *First, when she found out all that Amber was going through, she could have encouraged Amber to talk to the school counselor or another trusted adult. For the upcoming test, she could have gone with Amber to talk to the math teacher and given her support while asking the teacher for help.*
- What if you cheat and don't get caught? Is it okay then? *No, it's equally wrong regardless of whether or not you get caught—it's the action that's wrong, not the consequences.*
- Are there peer pressure situations that would not be very hard to resist because of your beliefs? (You'll probably get a wide variety of responses here.)
- What are some situations where you might be more pressured because your beliefs aren't as strong?

Explain that we all hold strong beliefs about some issues, and we tend not to be very tempted when people pressure us to do those things. In other situations, though, we need some help in figuring out how to live out our beliefs. Let's find out how to apply what you believe to specific peer pressure situations . . .

APPLY

Option 1: Drawing the Line. For this option, you need copies of "Drawing the Line" (found on the next page) and pens or pencils.

Distribute "Drawing the Line" and pens or pencils and explain that in many peer pressure situations, we need to decide ahead of time where we will draw the line—we need to decide what our beliefs will and will not allow us to do.

Instruct students to draw a line under the statements that best show what they believe; then put a star by the statements that best summarize what they think God would say.

If your group has a high level of trust with each other, have students share what they've underlined; otherwise, let them keep their answers to themselves. In any case, encourage them to keep their handouts and to look at them during the week to remind themselves of where they are drawing the line in their lives.

Drawing the Line

Underline a statement in each category that best represents what you believe. Draw a star next to a statement in each category that best represents what you think God would say.

Premarital Sex
When dating someone . . .
You should never touch each other.
It's okay to hold hands.
It's okay to kiss.
It's okay to kiss deeply.
It's okay to pet.
It's okay to have sexual intercourse.

Drinking
It's never okay to drink.
It's okay to drink only if you are of legal age.
It's okay for minors to drink if your parents give it to you.
It's okay to drink at any age.

Movies
While still in junior high . . .
It's okay to go to G-rated movies.
It's okay to go to PG movies.
It's okay to go to PG-13 movies.
It's okay to go to R-rated movies with your parents' permission.
It's okay to go to R-rated movies without your parents' permission.
It's okay to go to NC-17 movies.

Lying
It's never okay to lie.
It's okay to tell little white lies.
It's okay to lie if the truth will hurt someone's feelings.
It's okay to lie if you are helping a friend.
It's okay to lie if it gets you out of trouble.
It's okay to lie for any reason.

Dare to Be Different!

Suggestion: Since this session is about convictions and beliefs, use this opportunity to share the message of the gospel. Invite anyone who hasn't already done so to invite Jesus into his or her life as Lord and Savior right now! Close in prayer, thanking God for His tremendous love for every one of His children and asking Him to help students stand firm in their beliefs in the coming weeks.

Option 2: Moral Dilemmas. For this option, you need one copy of "Moral Dilemmas" (found on the next page). Ahead of time, cut the handout into four separate dilemmas.

Explain that we all face situations in our lives when our beliefs will be challenged and we won't know what to do. These moral dilemmas sometimes come in the form of negative peer pressure, where a bunch of people are pressuring us to do something questionable. If we really know who we are and what we believe when we face these situations, we should know what to do.

Divide students into four groups and distribute one moral dilemma to each group. Instruct groups to come up with some advice for the person in their assigned situation. Allow a few minutes for discussion; then regroup and discuss what each group came up with. If you have time, probe into what the person in each situation would gain—or lose—by following the groups' recommendations.

Close in prayer, thanking God for His tremendous love for every one of His children and asking Him to help students stand firm in their beliefs in the coming weeks.

Youth Leader Tip

Many students today are completely broken down mentally, physically and spiritually because they have never understood or experienced God's forgiveness. Help students to understand the fact that confessed sin is forever forgiven.[2]

Moral Dilemmas

Dilemma 1

A man borrows his neighbor's hunting rifle, promising to return it if his neighbor wants to use it. One day the neighbor, in a fit of rage, asks for the gun—apparently with the intention to kill someone. The man is faced with a dilemma: He can keep his promise and take a chance on being an accessory to a murder or he can break his promise and possibly save the neighbor from doing something he might regret. What should the man do?

Dilemma 2

Ben has just started dating Kristen. One night, Ben goes to Kristen's house to pick her up for a dance. When she comes downstairs, she spins around and asks, "What do you think of my new outfit?" Ben thinks the outfit is really ugly. What should he say?

Dilemma 3

Brittany went over to Amy's house to watch a video. Even though her parents told her they didn't want her watching R-rated movies, Brittany watched the one Amy's brother rented anyway. When she got home, her parents asked her what movie they watched. What should she say?

Dilemma 4

Michael is at an amusement park with his friends and loses his wallet and all of his money. His friends don't have enough money to lend him any for lunch. While waiting in line for a ride, Michael sees a wallet on the ground. He picks it up and sees that it has $30 in it, but no identification. What should he do?

REFLECT

The following short devotions are for the students to reflect on and answer during the week. You can make a copy of these pages and distribute to your class or print out from the PDF available online at **www.gospellight.com/un common/uncommon_jh_friends_and_peer_pressure.zip.**

1—WHO DOES GOD THINK YOU ARE?

Wander over to Ephesians 1:3-4.

Who do you think you are?

"My friends tell me that I am the prettiest girl they know," one eighth-grader says.

"I am a student," says another.

"I am John and Judy's son" or "I am a crocodile hunter," two other students might say.

Sometimes the way we see ourselves depends on things that we do (in the case of the crocodile hunter) or the people we are related to (in the case of John and Judy's son) or even what others say about us (in the case of the eighth-grade beauty queen). But with all of the things we believe about ourselves and with all of the things that others tell us about ourselves, do we hear what God says about who we are? Who does God think you are?

Read Ephesians 1:3-4 out loud. In every place in the passage that has the words "us" or "we," put your name instead. Write out parts of the passage or the whole thing with your name to remind you of who you are!

Okay, given what you've just read in Ephesians, what two things should be different about your day?

_____

_____

_____

_____

_____

_____

_____

_____

Pray that God will help those two things to happen!

2—YOU ARE CHOSEN!

Turn to 1 Peter 2:9-10.

You run out onto the playground. Your heart pounds and your feet sweat. Bill and Ted are the two team captains, and they start calling names out for the kickball game. Will you be chosen?

Each of us knows the feeling of being chosen or being left out of a game or event. The good news is that God has already chosen each of us, and nobody is left out unless they choose to not respond to God's choice of them.

After you are chosen to be a part of a team, what are some of the responsibilities of being a part of that team?

_____

_____

_____

_____

_____

_____

_____

Being chosen by God is kind of like being on a team. What is one big responsibility that you can take on and do this week as a part of God's team?

_____

_____

_____

_____

_____

_____

3—ALIENATED

Go back to familiar territory and find 1 Peter 2:11.

Aliens are little greenish people with weird-looking faces who come to other planets to abduct humans for painful and gross experiments back on their own planets, right? Well, according to the verse you just read, aliens are actually a lot more like us than we think.

According to this passage, who are aliens?

_____

_____

_____

_____

_____

What a weird thought, huh? People who follow Jesus (that's you and me!) are "aliens and strangers in this world"? The point is that we are different from regular earthlings because we follow Jesus.

Think of three ways that you are an alien (or three ways that you are different from the people around you because you follow Jesus).

_____

_____

_____

_____

What are two other things you feel you ought to do differently to be more like an alien in this world because you follow Jesus?

_____

_____

_____

_____

_____

Now go do those two things!

4—UNCOOL

Kevin couldn't believe what was happening to him. The least-popular girl in the whole school, Melissa, got paired up with him for a huge science project. That meant Kevin would have to be working with Melissa every day for 53 minutes for the next six weeks. The rest of Kevin's friends ended up with cool partners, but Kevin ended up with the only girl in the whole class who wore the same outfit every day and only washed her hair every two weeks.

If Kevin wanted to practice Philippians 2:1-4 in his science class, what would he do?

- ❑ Rig an experiment so that it throws goo all over her and then join the rest of the class in laughing at her
- ❑ Get to know Melissa and find at least one thing he can appreciate about her
- ❑ Pretend to be sick, so he'd spend more time in the nurse's office than in science

Kevin's in a tough place—torn between what everybody else will think and Melissa's feelings. But imagine how different your school would be if everybody else treated others as more important than themselves.

Name one person in your school who often gets made fun of. What can you do this week to show that you consider that person better than yourself?

_____

_____

_____

_____

_____

_____

PERSONAL PURITY

As a seventh-grader walking to the school cafeteria, I couldn't believe my eyes. On the fence near the gym, there hung a new brightly painted banner: "Come try our new cafeteria hamburgers. Now 100% beef."

I kid you not. That's what it said.

That started all sorts of rumors. If the burgers were now 100-percent beef, what had they been made of before? Vegetables? Frogs? Dogs?

We didn't know, and to be honest, we didn't want to know. But let's just say I started taking my own lunch from that point on.

See, what I wanted was to know that every hamburger that had ever been made in that cafeteria was 100-percent beef. Pure beef. Nothing else added.

And that's really what it means to be pure—to be 100 percent of one thing. Being 95 percent doesn't cut it. It has to be 100 percent to be pure.

I once heard about this eighth-grader, Danny, who decided to be 100-percent purely dedicated to God. He knew that this meant he had to stay away from gossip, being mean to others, pornography on the Internet, and a whole bunch of other temptations.

There was one temptation that almost got the best of Danny: His friend, George, had an older brother who had had the same science teacher two years earlier. This teacher was pretty lazy, so he gave the same tests year after year. George had copies of all of his brother's tests and soon started handing them out ahead of time to his friends.

So Danny had a choice: either accept the copy that George was offering and get an *A* for sure or try to take the test on his own and get a *C* like always.

Before I tell you what he did, what would you do? Would you accept the test, telling yourself everybody else is doing it—besides, what's the big deal about a test?—or would you remain 100-percent dedicated to God and do the right thing?

Well, Danny decided to take the test on his own, and get this: He did better than anybody else on the test. Instead of just an *A*, he got an *A-plus*!

The story of Danny is a true one, but like they say in TV shows, "Some details have been changed to protect the innocent." It's actually a story from the Bible. Daniel 1 to be exact. There was no science test that Danny (a.k.a. Daniel) faced, but instead, he had to choose whether he would defile himself by eating the royal food and wine, which, although tasty, had been partially offered to idols. Daniel could have said to himself, *It's no big deal. It's only a little meal here and there, and my, don't those steaks look scrumptious.* Instead, he remained pure, eating vegetables and drinking water. At the end of 10 days, Daniel actually looked healthier and better nourished than the young men who ate the royal food.

There are a few lessons we learn from the story of Daniel. And if you want to remain pure in a world that is tempting you with hatred, violence, sex, alcohol, drugs and pretty much every sin that you can imagine, you might want to pay attention to them.

Little Choices Matter

A meal here, a meal there. A science test here, a science test there. They all seem like they're no big deal, but every time you make a wrong choice, you become less than 100-percent set apart for God.

Imagine your life is a circle like a hamburger patty (or if you're more in the mood for dessert, a pie). What percent of the circle is dedicated to God? Be honest now. What percent of the circle is dedicated to doing what you want to? What percent is dedicated to doing what others want you to do? The little choices you make along the way are like pieces out of that circle that make it less and less dedicated to God.

Flee Temptation

My hunch is that Daniel didn't stick around the kitchen when the royal food was being prepared, smelling it and wishing he could have some. That would only make it harder for him to say no when the time came.

The same is true for us today. If you figure out that something is tempting you and may make you less than 100-percent pure, get away from it. Run. Flee. Skeedaddle out of there. Remember the vivid picture painted in Proverbs 26:11: "As a dog returns to its vomit, so a fool repeats his folly." Gross.

Join Forces

If you read Daniel 1, you'll see that Daniel wasn't alone in making the choice to be 100-percent dedicated to God. He had three friends with him: Shadrach, Meshach and Abednego (of fiery furnace fame). All four of the friends refused to eat the unholy food and all four were served the same simple meals. I'll bet it gave Daniel a bunch of comfort and courage when he looked over and saw Shadrach and Abednego eating the same broccoli and carrots that he was.

Hook up with other Christians on your campus or keep in close touch with friends from church when you're making those tough decisions. There's power in numbers—especially since one of those on your side is God!

ENDNOTES

Session 1: Building Friendships
1. Saul was jealous of David because of a song he heard the women singing after David killed Goliath: "Saul has slain his thousands, David his tens of thousands" (1 Samuel 18-7-8). Yet in Hebrew poetry, although the song suggests that David's deeds were greater, this was a common way of saying, "Saul and David have both slain thousands."

Session 2: Strengthening Friendships
1. In 1 Samuel 20:13, Jonathan's blessing to David, "May the Lord be with you as he has been with my father," indicates that God had revealed to Jonathan that David would be the next king—even though he, the current king's son, was expected to assume the throne. Jonathan is such a good friend that he is willing to put aside his own interests to do what is best for both David and the Israelites.

Session 3: Serving Our Friends
1. Kara Eckman Powell, *What Is Love?* (Ventura, CA: Gospel Light, 1998), p. 14.

Session 4: Gossip
1. Kara Eckmann Powell, *God's Plan for You* (Ventura, CA: Gospel Light, 1998), p. 51.
2. Kara Eckmann Powell, *Fear Not!* (Ventura, CA: Gospel Light, 1997), p. 54.

Session 5: Jealousy
1. Kara Eckmann Powell, *Fear Not!* (Ventura, CA: Gospel Light, 1997), p. 28.
2. First Samuel 18:10 states that an "evil spirit came forcefully upon Saul." Likewise, 1 Samuel 16:14 states, "an evil spirit from the Lord tormented him." These statements and other passages in Scripture suggest that evil spirits are under God's rule and can only operate within His predetermined boundaries. This doesn't mean that God sends evil spirits, however, as that would be against His nature.
3. Kara Eckmann Powell, *What Is Love?* (Ventura, CA: Gospel Light, 1998), p. 30.

Session 6: Unresolved Anger
1. Kara Eckmann Powell, *Fear Not!* (Ventura, CA: Gospel Light, 1997), p. 40.
2. Kara Eckmann Powell, *God Knows You're Talented* (Ventura, CA: Gospel Light, 1999), p. 49.

Session 7: Standing Firm
1. Jim Burns, *Uncommon Youth Ministry* (Ventura, CA: Gospel Light, 2001), p. 243.
2. The image that Nebuchadnezzar erected in Babylon may not have been a statue. The Aramaic word translated as "image" (*selem*) usually meant it had some human form, but not always. The dimensions given in Daniel 3 suggest that the image was 90 feet high and 9 feet wide. This 10-to-1 ratio doesn't fit the standard dimensions of the human body. This leaves two possibilities: (1) the image was placed on a pedestal to make it more impressive, or (2) it was similar to an Egyptian obelisk. It is possible that Nebuchadnezzar had been to Egypt, seen one and wanted something like it for his kingdom.

Session 8: Beware and Be Wise
1. "Potiphar" literally means "one devoted to the sun." This could mean that Potiphar lived in Heliopolis, a city in the Nile delta bordering Canaan, which was devoted to worship of the sun god. In Genesis 39:1, Potiphar is also listed as being "captain of the guard." This could mean chief cook or chief inspector of the plantations, but most believe it means that he was the chief executioner.
2. Jim Burns, *Uncommon Youth Ministry* (Ventura, CA: Gospel Light, 2001), p. 244.

Session 9: Get Your Ears on Straight
1. Jim Burns, *Uncommon Youth Ministry* (Ventura, CA: Gospel Light, 2001), p. 250.

Session 10: Go by the Book
1. Many people believe that the reason Jesus fasted for 40 days prior to being tempted in the wilderness was so that Satan's temptation to turn stones into bread would be even greater to Him because He was so weak. However, it is also possible that the Spirit had Him fast for 40 days to make Him stronger. Jesus had been denying His personal desires for 40 days, which might have made it easier for Him to resist those temptations when Satan came along.

Session 11: Plug in to Real Power
1. Adapted from Jim Burns, general editor, *Uncommon Games and Icebreakers* (Ventura, CA: Gospel Light, 2008), p. 151.
2. Jim Burns, *Uncommon Youth Ministry* (Ventura, CA: Gospel Light, 2001), p. 248.

Session 12: Stand or Fall
1. Jim Burns, *Uncommon Youth Ministry* (Ventura, CA: Gospel Light, 2001), p. 256.
2. Ibid., p. 257.

More *Uncommon*
Resources for Leaders